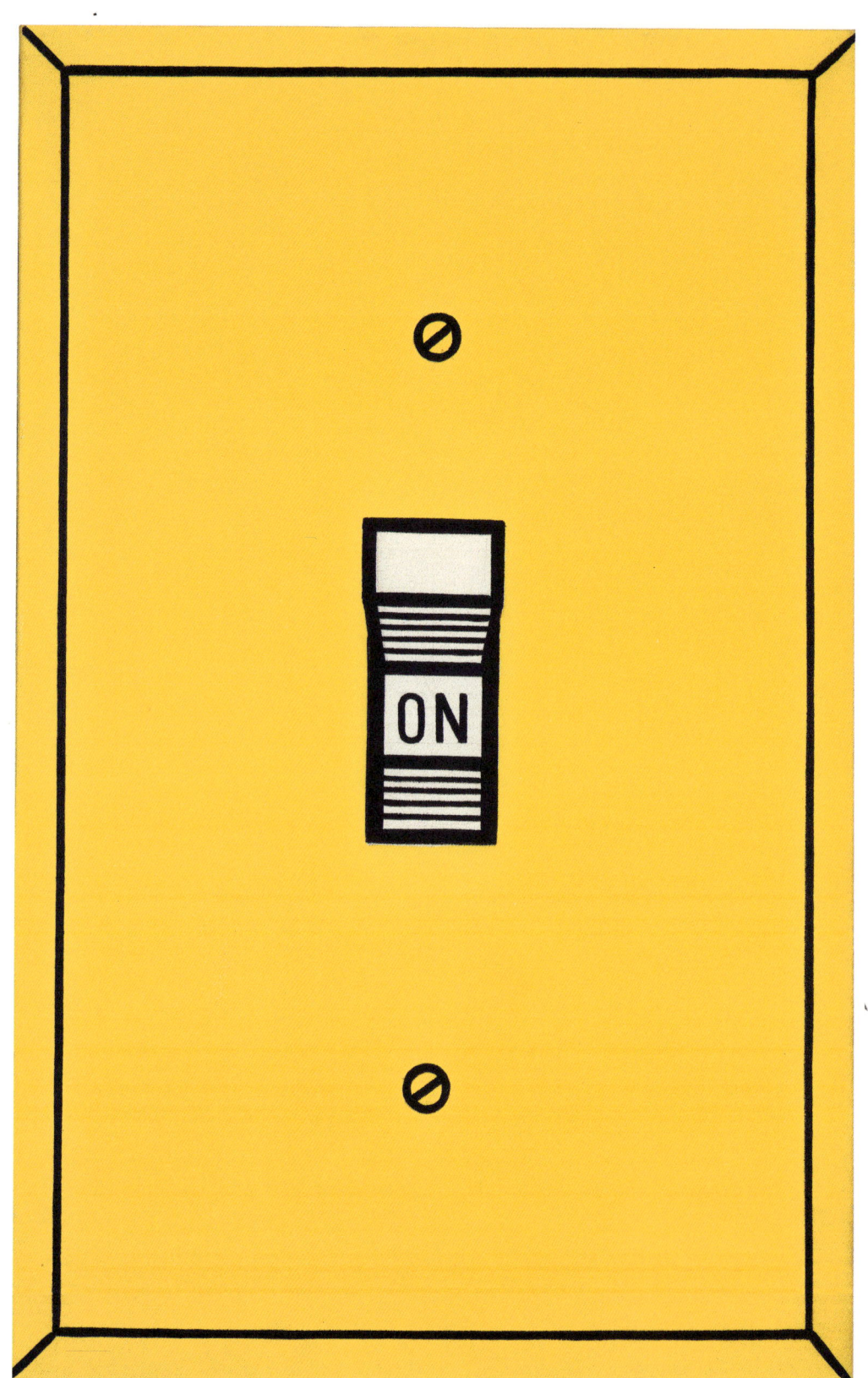

Roy Lichtenstein, *On*, 1961, oil on canvas, 29 × 19 in., Collection Simonyi

—POP DEP— —ART URES

Catharina Manchanda

With contributions by
Ken Allan | Anne Ellegood | Elodie Evers | Hal Foster
Lynn Hershman Leeson | Josephine Meckseper | Richard Meyer
Mickalene Thomas | James Voorhies

Published by the Seattle Art Museum in association with
Yale University Press, New Haven and London

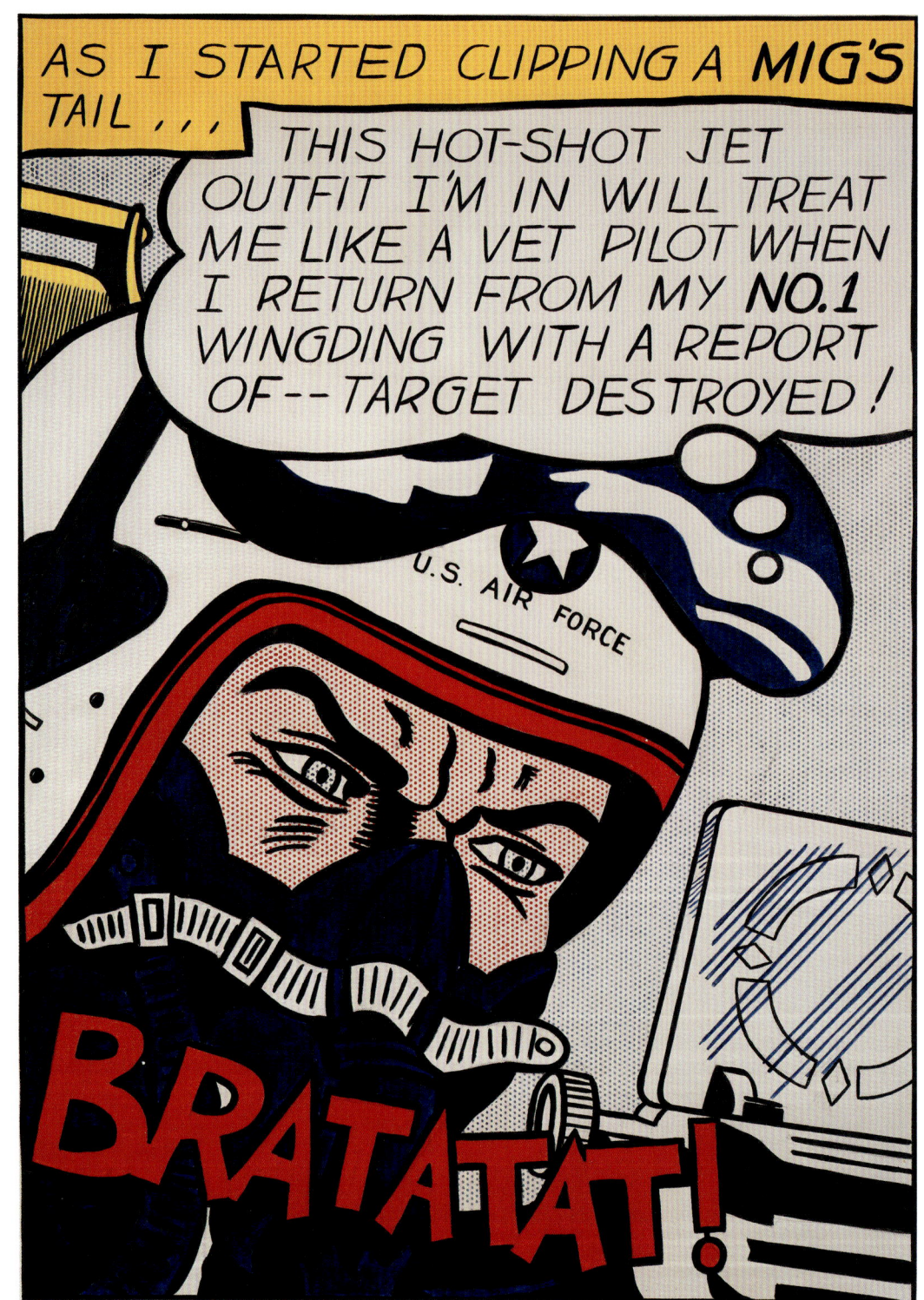

Roy Lichtenstein, *Bratatat*, 1962, magna on canvas, 46 × 34 in., Collection Simonyi

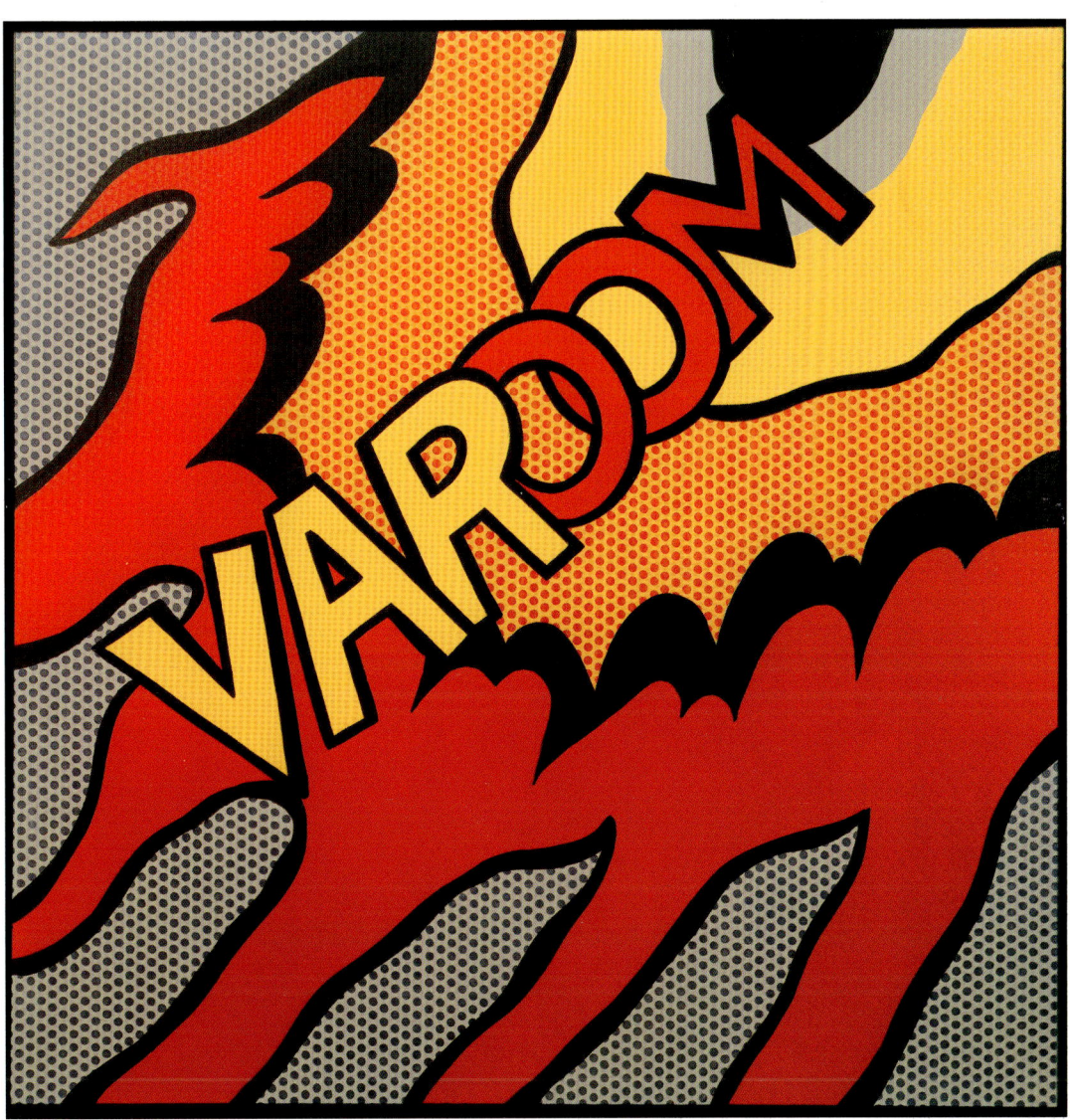

Roy Lichtenstein, *Varoom*, 1965, oil and magna on canvas, 36 × 36 in., Collection Simonyi

Contents

7
DIRECTOR'S FOREWORD & ACKNOWLEDGMENTS
Kimerly Rorschach

11
POP DEPARTURES
Catharina Manchanda

35
GUEST COMMENTARY

97
SUGGESTED READING

100
GUEST CONTRIBUTORS

101
EXHIBITION CHECKLIST

35
HAL FOSTER
37
RICHARD MEYER
39
MICKALENE THOMAS

55
KEN ALLAN
57
JOSEPHINE MECKSEPER
59
JAMES VOORHIES

79
LYNN HERSHMAN LEESON
81
ANNE ELLEGOOD
83
ELODIE EVERS

DIRECTOR'S FOREWORD & ACKNOWLEDGMENTS

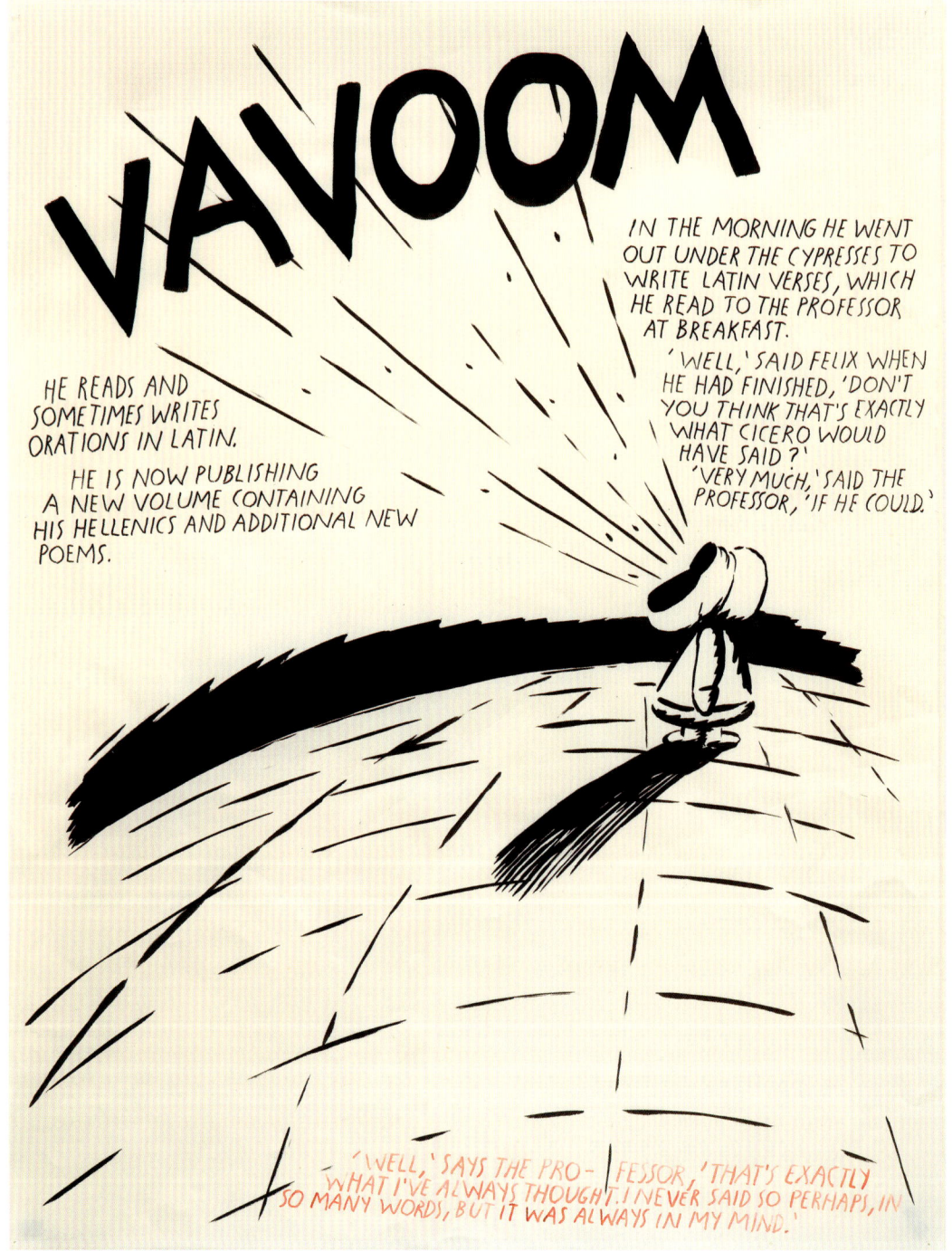

Raymond Pettibon, *No Title (Vavoom in the)*, 1991, ink on paper, 20⅞ × 17 in., courtesy of the artist and Regen Projects, Los Angeles

Kimerly Rorschach
Illsley Ball Nordstrom Director and CEO

Director's Foreword & Acknowledgments

More than fifty years after American pop art made its debut in the early 1960s, the provocative ideas that Roy Lichtenstein, Claes Oldenburg, Edward Ruscha, James Rosenquist, Andy Warhol, and their peers first introduced are still reverberating in contemporary art and culture. With pop art, consumerism and the image culture surrounding it were put on bold display, and many artists rebelled against traditional notions of artistic style through their retooling and imitation of commercial printing techniques. Initially greeted with amusement and outrage by the art world, pop art today is recognized as a foundation for subsequent artistic developments and critical discussions on many levels. This exhibition investigates how artists in subsequent decades have continued to critically engage with and redefine consumer culture and the cult of celebrity. We begin with the pioneering moment of the 1960s and continue into the 1980s and 1990s, when artists focused on the role of photography as marketing, consumption, and the media landscape were all undergoing profound changes. The exhibition extends to the present with crucial work made in the last ten years, as artists considered and reacted to technological developments that further reconfigured modes of both communication and consumption.

When the artworks are installed, an exhibition becomes a space for exploration. Our particular gratitude is to all the artists, whose compelling work prompts us to think more deeply about consumer culture and how it has informed contemporary art practices since the 1960s. This exhibition brings together pivotal work from each period and was made possible by the remarkable generosity of artists, private collectors, museums, and galleries in the United States and Europe. Many individuals and institutions lent seminal works from their collections, and we are profoundly thankful for their generous help. I would especially like to thank the Seattle community of collectors who rallied to support us and parted with treasured works, many of them outstanding examples of the pioneering pop period.

In order to broaden the platform for discussion, we invited nine artists, scholars, and curators to contribute their own views and questions regarding the issues the exhibition examines. For sharing their insights and perspectives, our thanks go to artists Lynn Hershman Leeson, Josephine Meckseper, and Mickalene Thomas; scholars and critics Ken Allan, Associate Professor of Art History at Seattle University; Hal Foster, Townsend Martin Class of 1917 Professor of Art & Archaeology at Princeton University; and Richard Meyer, Robert and Ruth Halperin Professor in Art History at Stanford University; as well as to museum professionals Anne Ellegood, Senior Curator at the Hammer Museum in Los Angeles; Elodie Evers, Curator at the Kunsthalle Düsseldorf; and

DIRECTOR'S FOREWORD & ACKNOWLEDGMENTS

James Voorhies, John R. and Barbara Robinson Family Director of the Carpenter Center for the Visual Arts at Harvard University.

An exhibition of this scale requires substantial financial support from a broad spectrum of private, public, and corporate donors. *Pop Departures* is supported by a domestic indemnity from the Federal Council on the Arts and the Humanities. It is made possible by the generosity of all the donors to Phase Two of the Seattle Art Museum's Fund for Special Exhibitions, whose dedication to this museum allows us to dream big. Presenting sponsors are The Boeing Company and Microsoft, which have been key supporters of the Seattle Art Museum for many years, and the mighty group of Seattle Art Museum Supporters (SAMS), who are tireless advocates for the museum's programs and exhibitions. 4Culture provides valuable local government support for the arts. Sponsorship for this exhibition is also generously provided by Phillips auction house. We are deeply grateful to our official airline sponsor, Delta Air Lines. Lastly, we would like to thank our print media sponsor, *The Seattle Times*, which helps us spread the word to Seattle's diverse audiences.

I am also grateful to our experienced and talented Seattle Art Museum team, whose hard work and attention to detail makes it all possible. I am especially grateful to Curatorial Assistant Carrie Dedon, who coordinated the entire project, and Exhibitions Coordinator and Image Rights Administrator Megan Peterson, who oversaw all the image rights. My special appreciation goes to Susan Brotman Deputy Director for Art and Curator of European Painting and Sculpture Chiyo Ishikawa, Exhibitions and Publications Manager Zora Hutlova Foy, Director of Museum Services and Chief Registrar Lauren Mellon, Senior Registrar for Exhibitions Phil Stoiber, Chief Conservator Nicholas Dorman and Conservator Liz Brown, and Director of Exhibition Design Chris Manojlovic and his expert crew, as well as to Creative Services Consultant Kevin Schroer and his design team, and Curatorial Editor Sheryl Ball, who attended to all in-house graphics. A robust program of lectures and events for this exhibition was developed under the guidance of SAM's wonderful education team, led by Assistant Director of School and Educator Programs Regan Pro, Manager of Teen, Family, and Community Engagement Programs Sarah Bloom, and Manager of Public Programs Philip Nadasdy. Director of Public Relations and Marketing Cara Egan and her team oversaw our marketing and publicity efforts. I would also like to thank Erica Anderson for her beautiful catalogue design, Ann Bremner for her elegant and careful editorial work, and our colleagues at Marquand Books for their expert realization of this catalogue.

Lastly, and most importantly, I am enormously grateful to Catharina Manchanda, SAM's Jon and Mary Shirley Curator of Modern and Contemporary Art, who conceived the idea for this exhibition and its intriguing premise, and realized it brilliantly.

VISIONS OF THE NEW (YOU)

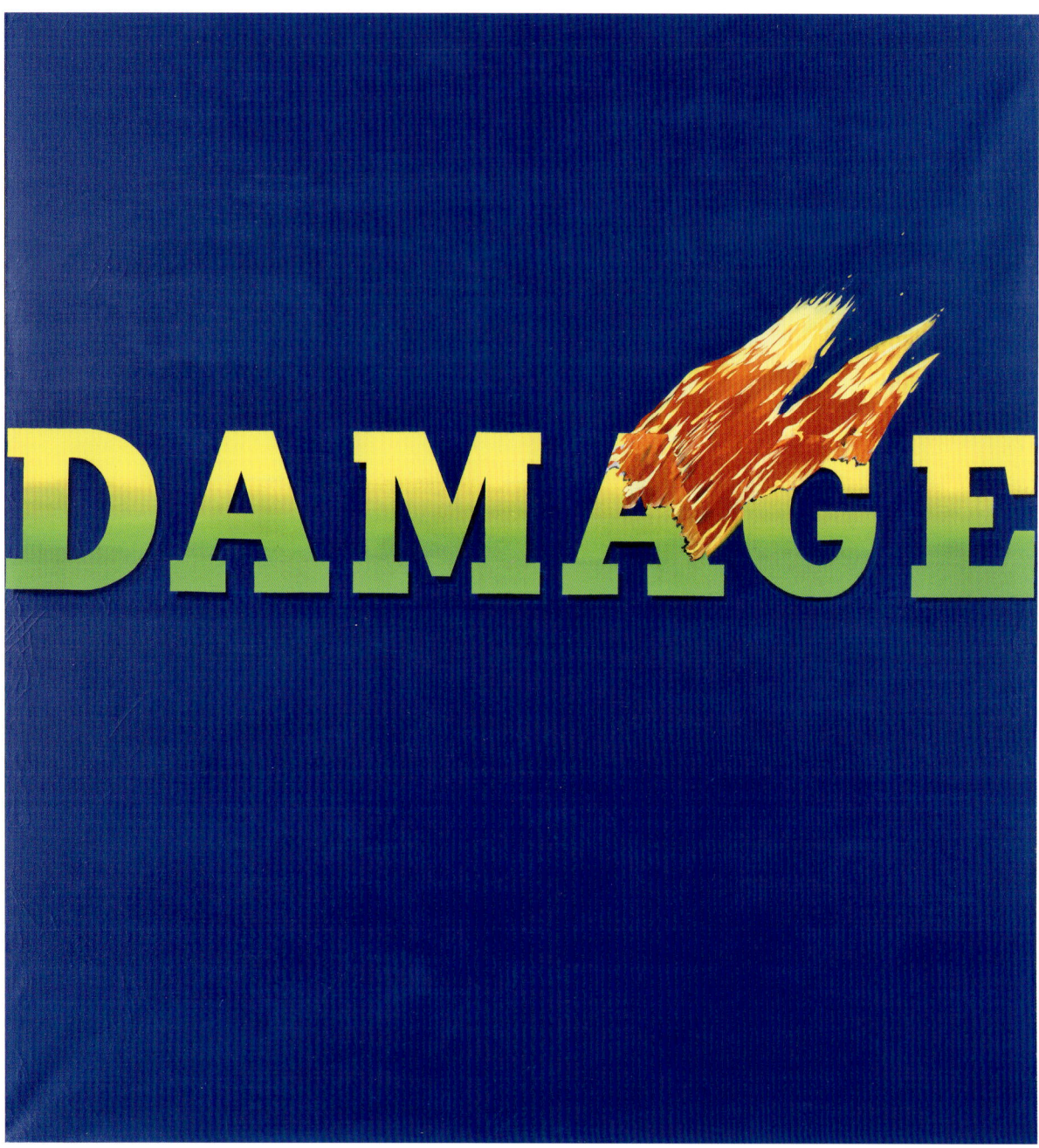

Ed Ruscha, *Damage*, 1964, oil on canvas, 72 × 67 in., Collection of Jeffrey and Susan Brotman

POP DEPARTURES

Catharina Manchanda

Jon & Mary Shirley Curator of Modern & Contemporary Art

Visions of the New (You)

At a time when most of Europe was still recovering from World War II, British artist Richard Hamilton marveled at the exotic optimism of American consumer culture in the 1950s. In an ironic collage he placed the sculpted physique of a bodybuilder and a shapely female at the heart of a modern home, whizzing with the latest gadgets, movie advertisements shining through a window, and hyperbolically posed the question *Just what is it that makes today's homes so different, so appealing?* (p. 12). Hamilton's broadside was the prelude to the phenomenon that became known as pop art.

Like Hamilton and his British peers, American artists reacted to a dramatically expanding postwar consumer landscape that reshaped everyday life. Except the visual culture of consumption was not a distant, exotic occurrence for them but everyday life. American pop art's focus on commodity culture allowed for a radical reassessment of cultural and artistic values and became the engine for artistic enquiries far into the future.

The *Pop Departures* exhibition centers on the topics of consumerism and display, as well as our ongoing infatuation with celebrity culture, all of which are bound up tightly with a constantly changing media and communications landscape. To better understand some of the shifts that have occurred since the 1960s, the exhibition highlights three artistic moments that center largely on developments in the United States. It features key works by pioneers of American pop art in the 1960s, followed by critical responses to popular culture imagery in the 1980s and early 1990s, and finally, contemporary artistic departures after the turn of the millennium. What made the image culture of consumption such a compelling topic? And how has the discussion shifted and eddied since classic pop art shattered dearly held ideals of artistic practice?[1]

---

1. In recent years, the urgency of pop art and its lasting impact have been felt in many quarters. Several major exhibitions have returned to aspects of pop art past and present, and the trend is continuing. Examples are *Pop Life: Art in a Material World* curated by Jack Bankowsky, Alison M. Gingeras, and Catherine Wood at Tate Modern, London, October 1, 2009–January 17, 2010, and *Regarding Warhol: Sixty Artists, Fifty Years* curated by Mark Rosenthal, Marla Prather, and Ian Alteveer at the Metropolitan Museum of Art, New York, September 18–December 31, 2012. Also in the works is *International Pop*, an exhibition curated by Darsie Alexander and Bartholomew Ryan, which will open at the Walker Art Center in spring 2015.

The artists of the 1960s reacted to a buoyant consumer society that had grown by leaps and bounds after World War II.[2] Cultural studies have emphasized the social mobility that fueled individual consumption at the time: "By the late 1950s, 20 percent of American families were pulling up stakes every year as homes became like cars, objects to be traded in."[3] The white middle class was the most active participant in this economic undertaking, but rapidly expanding access to television in the 1950s and early 1960s also introduced working-class families to the new dream of prosperity measured in goods. This relentlessly optimistic vision, which could be updated and upgraded at any time, was heavily marketed through all available media outlets.

No artist of the time was better positioned to understand the subtleties of marketing and the projection of desire than Andy Warhol. Born in the industrial city of Pittsburgh, Warhol was the youngest son of a family of recent immigrants from northern Slovakia. He was a first-generation American whose unlikely path propelled him within a few short years from his working-class surroundings in Pittsburgh to a glamorous career in New York. In the late 1950s, Warhol created magazine illustrations for the upper echelon of New York society and gained experience in decorating shop windows. He was already celebrated as a highly successful illustrator before launching himself as Warhol the artist, celebrity, filmmaker, artistic director, impresario, publisher, and self-styled pop icon.

An insightful essay by art historian Anthony Grudin reconsiders issues of class in Warhol's earliest paintings, whose images were often borrowed from tabloids, and retraces the source materials and their target audiences. He underscores the widespread popular appeal of superheroes and bodily perfection at the time and the power of these ideas for disadvantaged segments of society, but he also highlights how consumption was marketed as a form of cultural participation.[4] Self-reflective irony would occasionally surface in advertisements or comics, and Grudin sees in Warhol's early work an acknowledgment of the viewer as both indulgent participant and critic. Long before the current species of self-aware consumer emerged, Warhol himself certainly saw the marketing machine for what it was—an engine for creating desire, for self-improvement, using glamour and sex appeal as marketing tools. Warhol also understood how to play the world of highbrow art. He scandalized and intrigued New York's cultural elite by acting as the *enfant terrible* that re-presented the most profane consumer goods—boldly silkscreened on canvas—as desirable art as if an insider's joke. Rather than offering a slick sales pitch, Warhol cultivated the blasé manner of a dandy, described by Calvin Tomkins as "nebulous and passive."[5]

Looking toward our contemporary times, it is Warhol's fascination with celebrity culture—his reinvention of portraiture as celebrity icon and the creation of his own counterculture platform—that sets him apart from other New York pop artists. In a stroke of irreverence and genius Warhol renamed his studio the Factory and demystified artistic production through the suggestion that it is sheer assembly-line labor.

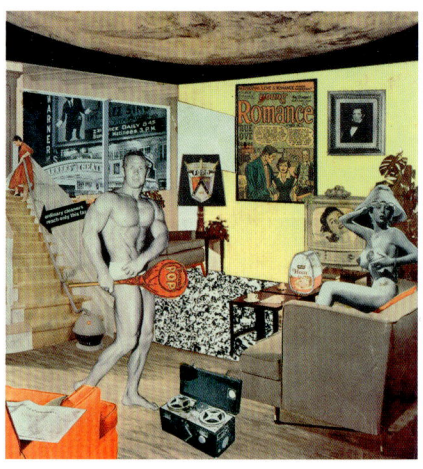

Richard Hamilton, *Just what is it that makes today's homes so different, so appealing?*, 1956, collage on paper, 10¼ × 9⅞ in., Kunsthalle Tübingen, Germany

2. Key artists who helped to define pop art lived and worked in New York: Andy Warhol, Roy Lichtenstein, James Rosenquist, Claes Oldenburg, John Chamberlain, and Tom Wesselmann. Notable exceptions are several California artists. Ed Ruscha reacted to both pop art and minimalism and also mined the aesthetics and structures of movies for his influential work. Wayne Thiebaud and Mel Ramos got to know each other at Sacramento State College, where Thiebaud taught, and both artists contributed key ideas to the larger pop phenomenon.
3. Gary Cross, *An All-Consuming Century: Why Commercialism Won in Modern America* (New York: Columbia University Press, 1993), 91.
4. Anthony E. Grudin, "'Except Like a Tracing': Defectiveness, Accuracy and Class in Early Warhol," *October*, Spring 2012, 162.
5. Calvin Tomkins, *Off the Wall: Robert Rauschenberg and the Art World of Our Time* (New York: Penguin Books, 1980), 176.

All the while, he successfully cultivated a new mystique that is no longer centered on the lone artist toiling in the studio but on a notion of studio practice as a club for artistic and social experimentation.

For all these reasons, Andy Warhol looms large in discussions of pop art in relation to contemporary artistic practice. But Warhol's particular enterprise has also distorted our understanding of 1960s pop and its complex cultural context. The catchy label would like to make us think of pop as one unified movement, but the artists who became associated with it worked independently and contributed unique perspectives and ideas.

If there is one unifying aspect in the diversity of 1960s pop art, it is the presentation of consumer goods and advertising imagery in painting and sculpture. Roy Lichtenstein, Andy Warhol, James Rosenquist, Tom Wesselmann, and Claes Oldenburg are just some of the pioneers who appropriated, altered, and re-presented consumer objects and images through painting and sculpture, often underscoring their seductiveness. In fact, the re-creation of media or television images in these artistic mediums helped to establish the dialectical tension between "high" and "low" and to articulate a critical discourse about image culture.[6]

The curator Henry Geldzahler retrospectively remarked, "Yet there was something brazen and joyful about Pop paintings that caused them to be read as enthusiastic (but sufficiently ironic) artifacts of the brave new world of the postwar era. . . . The question that was asked almost immediately in sophisticated art circles was, does this art glorify America, and is it simply a paean to consumerism?"[7] Magazine and television advertisements, product design and display, the billboard, the pin-up, and comic-strip imagery all found reflection in different pop art ventures. The banality and vulgarity of the subjects were much discussed but also seen as a productive foil against which American consumer society and the media world of images could be viewed in relief.

This point was especially argued for Roy Lichtenstein's work: "Like the machine-made creatures who use them, these objects are mass-produced forms of unforgettable ugliness. . . . Lichtenstein has found his content in a fresh examination of the shocking new commonplaces of modern experience that had previously been censored from the domain of art; and in that tradition, he has suddenly rendered visible what familiarity had prevented us from really seeing."[8] The esteemed critic Robert Rosenblum, who wrote this candid assessment in 1963, reacted to the heightened awareness of the reductivism and schematic fakeness of objects in Lichtenstein's work. The same reductivism extended to the constructions of action-driven masculinity that fuse man and machine and melodramatic models of femininity in the artist's adaptations of war and romance comics, a contrast that he heightened through subtle alterations in composition and text. Above all, his inclusion of direct speech and thought, and his visual conventions for rendering explosions or gunfire in bold graphics—BRATATAT! BOOM—placed these paintings, like a movie, in the here and now of the viewer's space.

6. See the catalogue of the exhibition *High & Low: Modern Art and Popular Culture* (New York: The Museum of Modern Art, 1990), which looked at the interchanges between art and popular culture, beginning with the collages of Picasso and Braque and ending with pop art. For a recent analysis of 1960s pop art painting and subjectivity, see Hal Foster's *The First Pop Age: Painting and Subjectivity in the Art of Hamilton, Lichtenstein, Warhol, Richter, and Ruscha* (Princeton: Princeton University Press, 2012).
7. Henry Geldzahler, "Introduction," *Pop Art 1955–1970* (New York: The Museum of Modern Art International Council, 1985), 14–15. From Geldzahler's perspective, it was the Vietnam War that forced a reconsideration of values, and pop art's images suddenly appeared far more complex.
8. Robert Rosenblum, "Roy Lichtenstein and the Realist Revolt," *Metro*, April 1963, reprinted in *Pop Art: A Critical History*, edited by Steven Henry Madoff (Berkeley: University of California Press, 1997), 193.

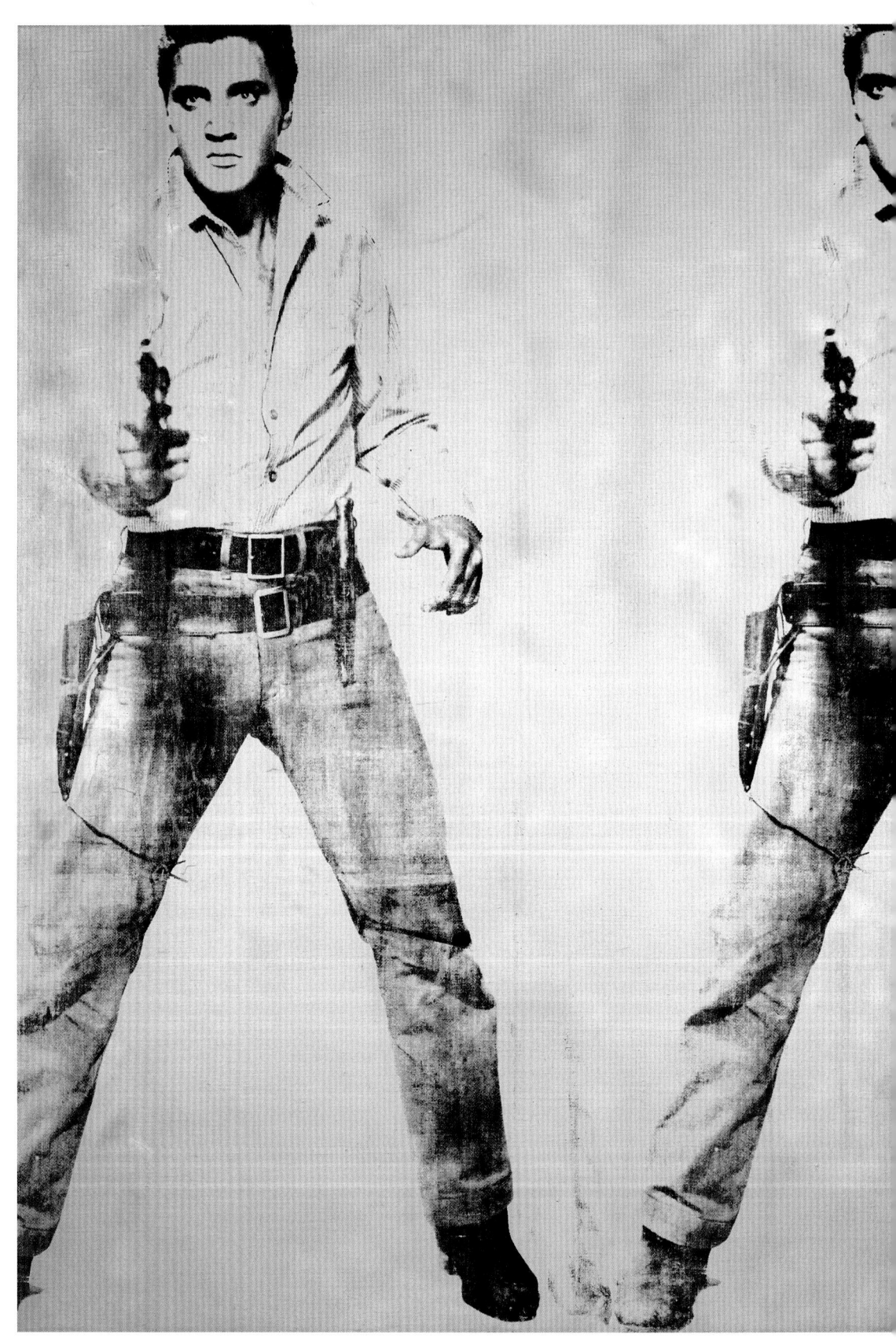

Andy Warhol, *Double Elvis*, 1963/ 1976, silkscreen ink, synthetic polymer paint on canvas, two panels, 82¼ × 59⅛ in. each, Seattle Art Museum, National Endowment for the Arts, PONCHO, and the Seattle Art Museum Guild, 76.9

The selected source material—comics from the immediate postwar period—would have separated these extreme gender stereotypes from changing roles and representations of them in the early 1960s. "One of the things a cartoon does," wrote Lichtenstein in 1968, "is to express violent emotion and passion in a completely mechanical and removed style. To express this thing in a 'painterly' style would dilute it. I want my images to be as critical, as threatening, and as insistent as possible."[9] His imitation of a "mechanical" style of reproduction became the logical extension of re-presenting these narrative models for contemporary viewers.[10] Consumption in these comic scenarios extends far beyond the supermarket shelf into more subtle psychological terrain. For Lichtenstein, subject matter includes constructions of individual subjectivity and identity within social and artistic norms.

Lichtenstein's comic-strip paintings from the early 1960s were made in tandem with other works that depicted schematic renditions of celebrated artistic styles. His red brushstroke reduced intuitive and individual expression into a set of graphic marks. Like an advertisement for Coca-Cola or Campbell's soup, the red brushstroke becomes a recognizable sign and critique of gestural painting and of a modernist notion of originality. Yet Lichtenstein consistently stages this departure through the use of paint and canvas.

Each of the pop artists mined a different aspect of commodity culture: Film stars, celebrity portraits, and product design were Warhol's chosen arena. Lichtenstein homed in on the visual language and subjects of comics. Rosenquist focused on the imagery of billboard advertisements in New York (a market that was increasingly squeezed by competition from television, in the same city). Tom Wesselmann reinvented the classic art historical odalisque in suburban settings as an empty surface. California-based Mel Ramos mashed advertisements and pin-up imagery into one, and Ed Ruscha in Los Angeles claimed the canvas as a movie screen and field for free word association.

Back in New York, Claes Oldenburg briefly converted his Lower East Side studio into a discount pop-up shop in 1961 and sold painted plaster casts of food items, clothing, and sundry items that could be found in adjacent neighborhood stores. The crammed nature of the store echoed the style of product display and retailing on the Lower East Side, which had a budget-conscious clientele. Presumably neither the goods nor the prices were particularly appealing to the working-class shoppers of the Lower East Side, except perhaps as a novelty, but artists, collectors, and critics came to see or purchase items for sale, and informed insiders started to write about the difference between the real and its representation. The near conflation of art and reality was noted in a 1963 review by Ellen H. Johnson. Oldenburg, she writes, "pushes the realism (and the humor) further by pricing [a slice of chocolate cake] in his 'Store' at $69.95 . . . and by his manner of presenting it: men's shirts and shorts in cardboard boxes, pastries in glass cases and on little serving dishes . . . this extreme realism makes more pungent the ironic realization that these are created objects: far from being sweet, sticky and melting, the cake is nasty, solid plaster."[11] A few years later,

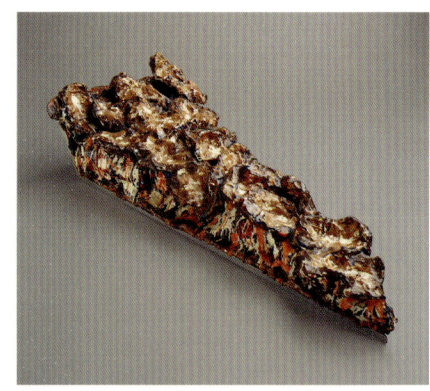

Claes Oldenburg, *Giant Wedge of Pecan Pie*, 1963, muslin soaked in plaster over wire frame, wood, painted with enamel, 15 × 21 × 50 in., Seattle Art Museum, Promised gift of the Virginia and Bagley Wright Collection, in honor of the 75th Anniversary of the Seattle Art Museum

9. Roy Lichtenstein, "Statements in the exhibition catalogue *Roy Lichtenstein*, London: The Tate Gallery, 1968," reprinted in Henry Geldzahler, *Pop Art 1955–1970*, 175.

10. Michael Lobel's detailed study of Lichtenstein offers a textured consideration of the individual's relationship to a mechanically reproduced culture. He studies the perceiving subject through the use of mechanical aids in Lichtenstein's compositions and the use of monocular vision as a vehicle for representing the relation between the body, vision, and the machine. Michael Lobel, *Image Duplicator: Roy Lichtenstein and the Emergence of Pop Art* (New Haven: Yale University Press, 2002).

11. Ellen H. Johnson, "The Living Object," *Art International*, January 1963, reprinted in *Pop Art: A Critical History*, 219–20. See also Cécile Whiting's "Shopping for Pop," a discussion of Oldenburg's store and critical reactions to it, in *A Taste for Pop: Pop Art, Gender and Consumer Culture* (Cambridge: Cambridge University Press, 1997), 7–49.

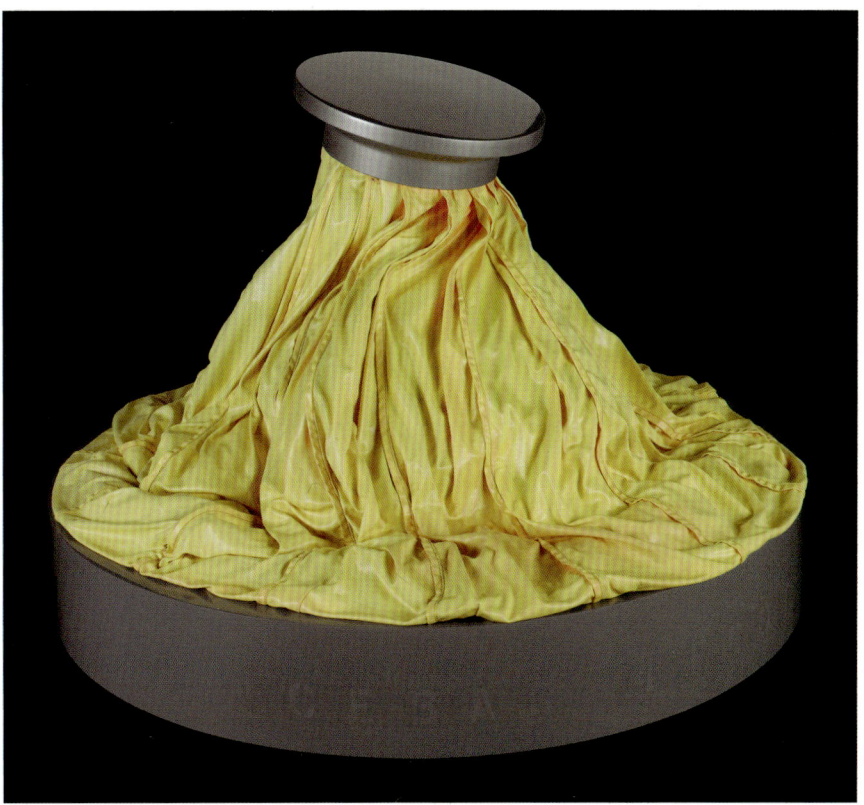

Claes Oldenburg, *Ice Bag–Scale B*, 1971, programmed kinetic construction in aluminum, steel, nylon, fiberglass, 40 × 48 × 48 in., Seattle Art Museum, Gift of Mr. and Mrs. David E. Skinner, II, 84.224

Oldenburg took his interest in commodities in a new direction when he collaborated with Patty Mucha, his wife at the time, on his first soft sculptures. The artist experimented with plain or painted canvas, and later with shiny vinyl, in works of often enormously inflated scale (his first hamburger sculpture was the size of a bed). Seduction is a familiar advertising strategy, and Oldenburg's oversized soft sculptures amplified this latent message. With a work such as his pneumatic *Ice Bag–Scale B* (this page), which gradually bulges and slumps, he recasts the humble household object with erotic suggestiveness.

In her study *A Taste for Pop*, Cécile Whiting makes a further connection between the analysis of commodities and displays by the artists and the way the work itself was staged. She singles out three atypical venues where pop art was inserted into a retail fabric in order to blur the boundaries between art and plain old shopping: the display of Andy Warhol's paintings in the Fifth Avenue shop windows of the high-end Bonwit Teller department store in April 1961, Claes Oldenburg's pop-up discount store on the Lower East Side in 1961, and a supermarket exhibition at the Bianchini Gallery on the Upper East Side in 1964, which inserted pop art into a temporary supermarket display (including Campbell's soup and other consumables).[12] Whiting stresses the play with class boundaries in each of these scenarios as an exercise in separating commodities from representations. And she retraces how these shows and the critical response to them also drew a distinction, between the everyday shopper and the culturally literate art connoisseur, which led to new considerations of visual culture.

12. See Cécile Whiting, "Shopping for Pop."

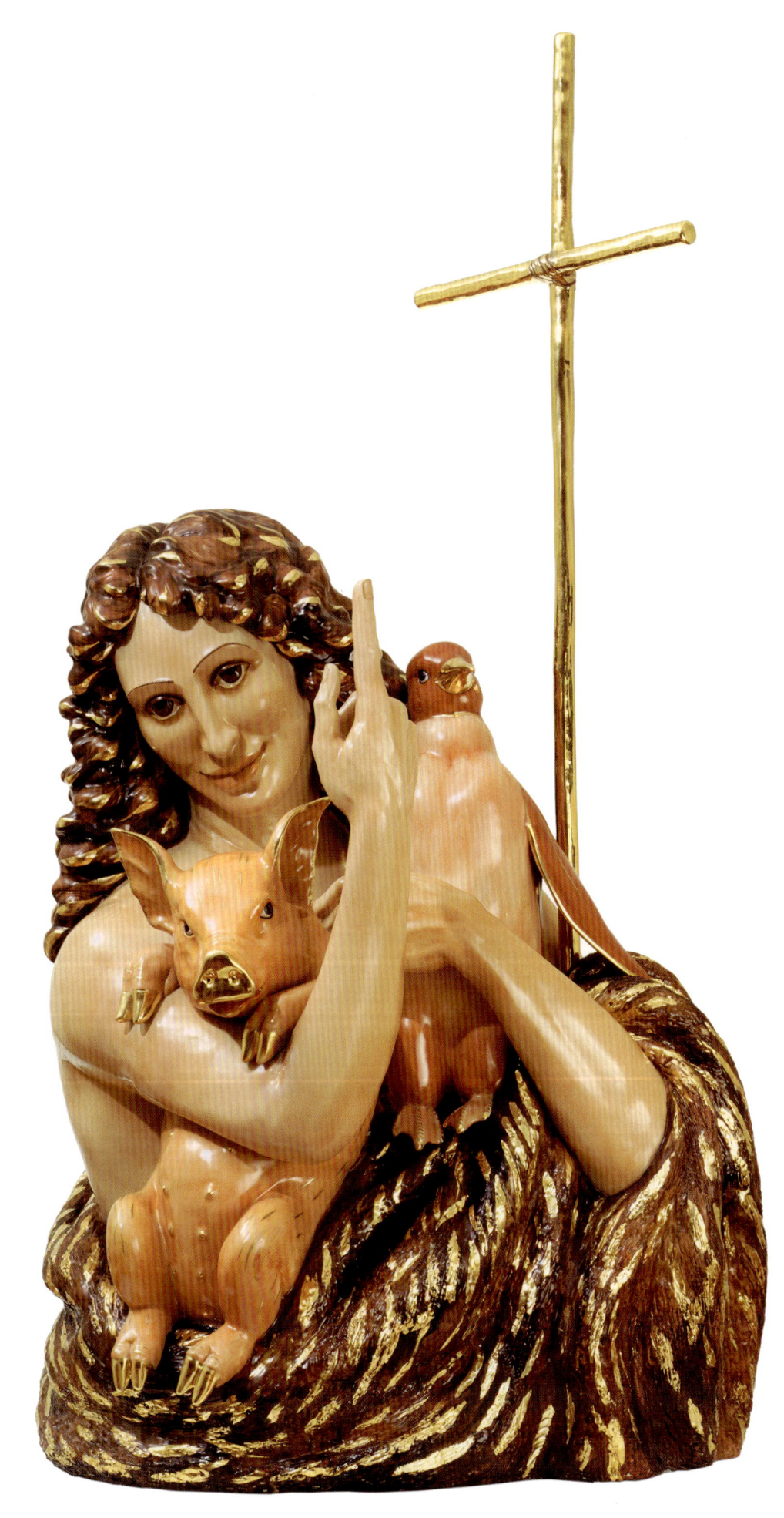

Living in a Material World

In the 1960s, pop artists began to consider popular culture imagery and consumer goods in a context of giddy consumer optimism (or, at least, projected optimism). In the 1980s and 1990s, many artists staked out a critical territory by claiming and manipulating media imagery in the face of growing conspicuous consumption that was no longer modeled on purchasing and furnishing the family home but centered instead on individual indulgence.

The body as commodity—which had figured prominently in Wesselmann's and Ramos's work—is a theme that connects to the next generation of artists. The treatment of the attractive female body as a fetishized object was an additional layer in the particular seduction of commodity images. As art historian and critic Hal Foster aptly noted: "Such is the theory of consumer capitalism that Pop implies: its political economy depends on a compounding of sexual, commodity, and semiotic fetishism, a 'super-fetishism' in which the making of products, images, and signs becomes evermore obscure while our investment in these phantoms becomes evermore intense."[13] Conceptual artists understood the photographic image in all its complexity as culturally and aesthetically coded. This was of particular significance to many women artists who developed techniques to stage and decode constructions of stereotypical beauty or feminine roles.[14]

New economic developments in the 1980s resulted in artists' renewed focus on commodity culture as the decade progressed. With the deregulation of markets in the Reagan era, commercialism and entertainment began to merge and the onslaught of advertisement became ever more relentless. Madonna's 1984 hit song "Material Girl" captures the hedonistic spirit of the moment:

Some boys kiss me, some boys hug me
I think they're O.K.
If they don't give me proper credit
I just walk away
They can beg and they can plead
But they can't see the light, that's right
'Cause the boy with the cold hard cash
Is always Mister Right, 'cause we are
Living in a material world
And I am a material girl.

The sentiment here is several shades colder and more transactional than in "Diamonds Are a Girl's Best Friend," as performed by Marilyn Monroe in the hit 1953 movie *Gentlemen Prefer Blondes*, on

---

Jeff Koons, *St. John the Baptist*, 1988, porcelain, 56½ × 30 × 24½ in., Seattle Art Museum, Gift of the Virginia and Bagley Wright Collection, in honor of the 75th Anniversary of the Seattle Art Museum, 2007.121

13. Hal Foster, *The First Pop Age*, 13.
14. For an overview of the feminist movement in art, including essays on the issue of photography, see the catalogue of the exhibition *WACK! Art and the Feminist Revolution*, organized by Cornelia Butler (Los Angeles: The Museum of Contemporary Art; Cambridge: MIT Press, 2007).

which Madonna modeled her song and her performance. Meanwhile, in the retail industry, significant changes took place in short succession: 1981 saw the creation of the Home Shopping Network; MTV launched the same year and quickly became a more subtle vehicle for a fusion of entertainment and sales. In addition, telemarketing increased significantly during the decade, and shopping itself was rebranded as a form of entertainment. A prominent example of this trend is the Mall of America, which opened in suburban Minneapolis in 1992 as the largest indoor mall in the country. It combined an amusement center, retailers, restaurants, and clubs and became a surprisingly popular tourist destination.[15]

The artistic departures in the 1980s were often predicated on a new, accelerated form of consumer culture, and artists increasingly used appropriated media images to investigate the image constructs and the power of representation.[16] Barbara Kruger's bold billboard-size works were informed by the feminist critiques and conceptual methods of the previous decades. She used formats and strategies familiar from advertising but added statements that irked and prompted a response. "I shop therefore I am," the text in one of her punchiest works from this period, turns any remnants of René Descartes' self-reflective humanist subject (in "I think therefore I am") into its opposite.

Richard Prince's appropriations, such as his cowboy series (opposite page) lifted from a Marlboro campaign, also targeted the world of advertising in the 1980s. Prince zeroed in on a form of advertisement that connected to a national mythology largely defined by Hollywood westerns. This campaign did not simply sell another cigarette but carried emotive weight. It was a marketing campaign that sold a romantic idea and lifestyle statement, and anachronistic as it was, it tapped into notions of American freedom, self-reliance, and independence that held widespread appeal.

A Forest of Signs: Art in the Crisis of Representation, Ann Goldstein and Mary Ann Jacob's insightful 1989 survey exhibition, contemplated these recent appropriation strategies. "During this Reagan era of the 1980s," wrote Jacobs in her introduction, "not just the art world, but art itself has changed. The dynamics of the art world are more intertwined than ever, and it is no wonder that art—imitating life—is now imitating life in the art world."[17] The exhibition focused on diverse forms of appropriation in commerce and advertising, and Jacobs observes that many works stand between criticality and complacency. Quoting the artist Jay Larsen, she poses the resonant question: "How valid is any critique of capitalism that aims at total success within the system?"[18]

Success within the system was certainly the goal for artist Jeff Koons, the great reveler in materialism in the 1980s. Banality and vulgarity were accusations already raised against pop art's subjects in the early 1960s, but Koons—who worked as a stock trader on Wall Street during the 1980s—fused kitsch and eroticism and cited Andy Warhol as an inspiration. His *Banality* exhibition in New York in 1989 brought together a different kind of folklore of industrial man: references to sacred and profane pleasures and desires were here given form on a

15. See Gary Gross's "Markets Triumphant, 1980–2000," chapter six in *An All-Consuming Century*, for a detailed account of the policy changes and repercussions in the world of media and marketing.
16. The collected writings of the art historian Craig Owens, published posthumously in a single volume in 1992, offered an influential look at the multifaceted subject of representation. See Craig Owens, *Beyond Recognition: Representation, Power, and Culture*, edited by Scott Bryson, Barbara Kruger, Lynne Tillman, and Jane Weinstock (Berkeley, Los Angeles, Oxford: University of California Press, 1992). Another significant publication of the time was the anthology *The Contest of Meaning: Critical Histories in Photography*, edited by Richard Bolton (Cambridge: MIT Press, 1989). Its essays by leading scholars analyzed the literal and culturally embedded meanings of photographic images, as well as the spaces in which they circulate.
17. Mary Jane Jacobs, "Art in the Age of Reagan: 1980–1988," in Ann Goldstein and Mary Jane Jacobs, *A Forest of Signs: Art in the Crisis of Representation* (Los Angeles: The Museum of Contemporary Art, and Cambridge: MIT Press, 1989), 19.
18. Ibid., 20.

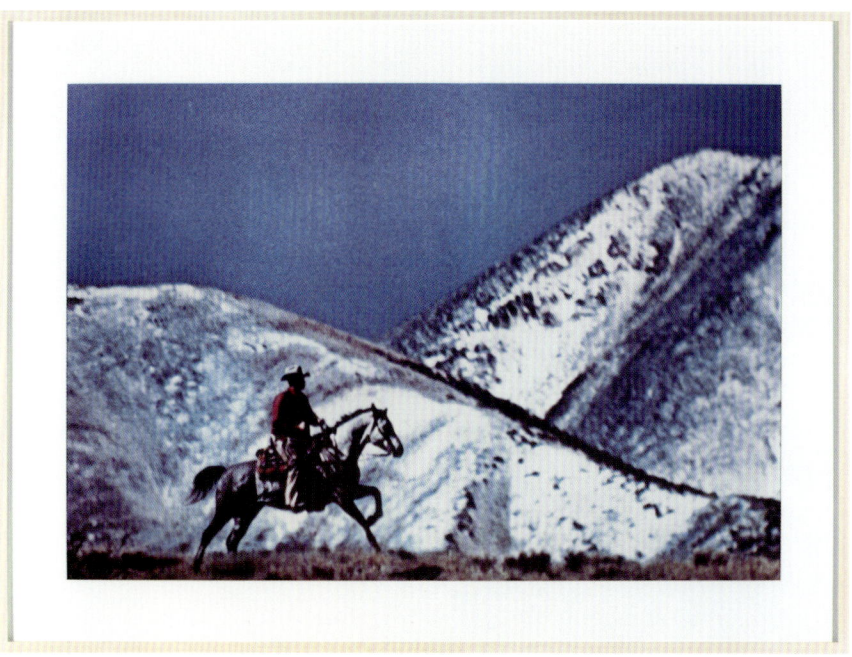

Richard Prince, *Untitled (Cowboys)*, 1980, Ektacolor print, 27 × 40 in., The Museum of Contemporary Art, Los Angeles, Purchased with funds provided by the National Endowment for the Arts, a Federal Agency, and Councilman Joel Wachs

19. As if speaking to a class of art students, Koons declares in a 1989 *Art and Design* interview, "The media is a phenomenon of communication that is something that should be embraced, whether you're using aspects of envy or whatever to communicate and stimulate the public. It's all very positive and you must use everything that's available to the best of your ability." He responds to pointed questions about his assumed artistic criticality with long-winded answers that project an air of carefully rehearsed, narcissistic naiveté. He says that he is unread and not cynical about the market, that he is working with things that are just "in the air." Koons wants to claim the mantle of Duchamp in his use of the readymade, but he expresses a guarded admiration for Warhol (who had died just two years before the interview was conducted). To Koons, Warhol, "communicate(s) intellectual information, not through a cerebral process but through a sexual process and this is why I have so much respect for him." Jeff Koons, "The Power of Seduction: An Art and Design Interview," reprinted in *New Art*, ed. Andreas Papadakis, Clare Farrow, and Nicola Hodges (New York: Rizzoli, 1991), 154.

large scale. Saccharine porcelain sculptures of a *Playboy* blonde hugging a pink panther that continued the pin-up traditions Mel Ramos had already mined for two decades, an enraptured St. John the Baptist pointing heavenward while holding not baby Jesus, but a pig and a penguin, and Michael Jackson and his pet chimpanzee, Bubbles, are but a few of the most prominent works Koons exhibited in this show (see pp. 18 and 65). Any vestiges of innocence suggested in the small kitsch souvenirs that served as reference points for this body of work were here revealed as flatfooted expressions of fantasy and desire. Koons's choice of subject and materials put bad taste on bold display, but the opulence of the material and finish had the pomp of rococo decadence.

As an artist, Koons embodied the hedonistic moment of the 1980s. He learned from Warhol in many respects, adopting the earlier artist's subject matter as well as his showmanship. Capitalizing on the new media and market mechanisms of the decade, he forged his own persona as a celebrity artist / pop star. Koons's choice of language in an interview from that time refers to sales strategies as an urgent need to "communicate" and echoes the blurring boundaries of retail and entertainment in American culture during this decade.[19] The artist's participation in a culture of excess, replicated in the materialization of kitsch or shiny bling in his sculptures, distinguishes him from image-based appropriation artists who aimed at a conceptual critique of media culture. By contrast, Koons's work immerses itself in the very glut and erotic thrill of consumption.

ALL-CONSUMED

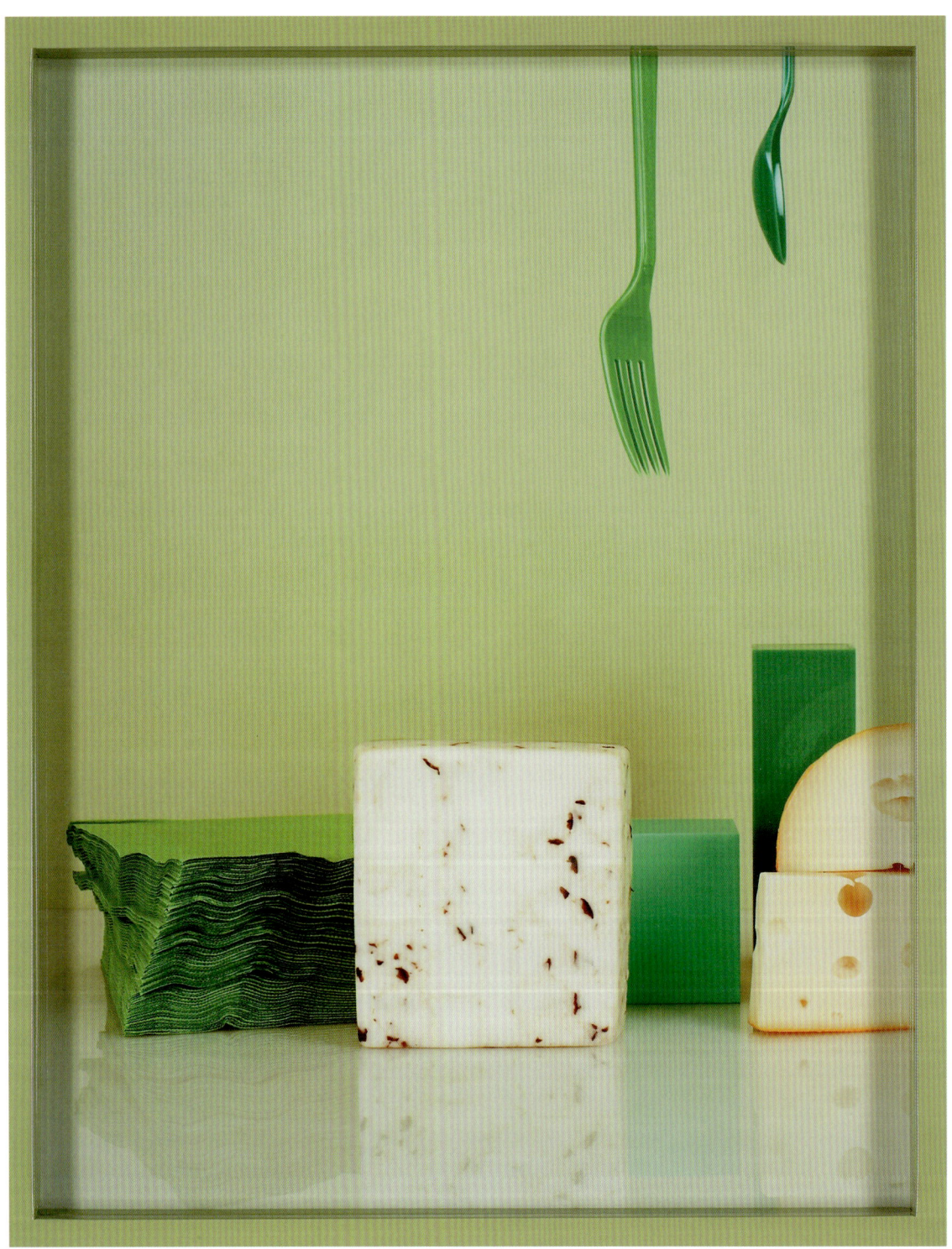

Elad Lassry, *Truffle Goat Cheese, Emmentaler, Fork and Spoon*, 2010, C-print, painted frame, 14 × 11½ × 1½ in., courtesy of David Kordansky and Mindy Shapiro, Los Angeles

All-Consumed

Cultural historian Marshall McLuhan's *Gutenberg Galaxy* of 1962 predicted the end of printed culture and the rise of computers, a shift in technology and communication that would profoundly reshape social structures on a global level. Written forty years before the Internet became available to the masses, McLuhan's text today reads like prophetic intuition. Two decades later, economist Theodore Levitt published an influential article for the *Harvard Business Review* that set the stage for the accelerated developments of the following decade. In his 1983 "The Globalization of Markets," Levitt observed that the differences between regional and national preferences were disappearing, allowing multinational companies to market and sell the same products worldwide. The 1990s became the decade when that predicted shift from analog to digital culture became mainstream, and technology became the tool for accelerated communication and trade. Especially since the turn of the millennium, the physical experience of shopping, including the stroll past shop windows and the perusal of goods in stores, has been increasingly replaced by online purchasing, aided by retailers and distributors such as Amazon. The *flâneur* of old is becoming a rarity, giving way to more solitary figures who operate at all hours from the comfort of their homes or the convenience of their offices. In the process, the image itself has gained a newly elevated status, as purchase decisions are no longer based on an examination of a product but of its image.

In this new technological moment, Jeff Koons's self-styled version of art stardom, modeled on Warhol, resonated with other contemporary artists. The trend of the "mega-artist," has continued ever since, despite political and financial crises.[20] The phenomenon also led to a renewed interest in Andy Warhol. In fact, just a few years before the millennial turn, Barbara Kruger's *Untitled (Not cruel enough)* (p. 69), pointed in this direction. Her large portrait of Warhol, whose image had become synonymous with glamour and celebrity, was framed by bold declarations that stood in opposition to the man's image: "Not cruel enough," "Not pathetic enough," "Not beautiful enough," "Not man enough," and lastly, "Not real enough," ran the commentary. In characteristic fashion, Kruger's work demonstrated the essential relationship between image and text, in this instance a battle over meanings that hold the entire work in constant tension. Kruger's work was made in 1997, ten years after the artist's death, at a time when Warhol's star was still rising. A few years later, the 2004 issue of the influential magazine *Artforum* was dedicated to "Pop After Pop"—and Warhol dominated the debates. A more focused look at the iconic art star in the vein of Warhol was the inspiration for the *Pop Life* exhibition organized by the Tate Modern in 2009. Jack Bankowsky, who had been the guest editor of the *Artforum* issue, begins his essay for the Tate catalogue noting, "Andy the publisher, Andy the gadfly, Andy the model and ad man and TV producer:

20. See Jonathan Jones, "Jeff Koons: Not just the king of kitsch," *The Guardian*, online archive, June 30, 2009. Damien Hirst and Takashi Murakami are two prominent contemporary artists who continue the trend.

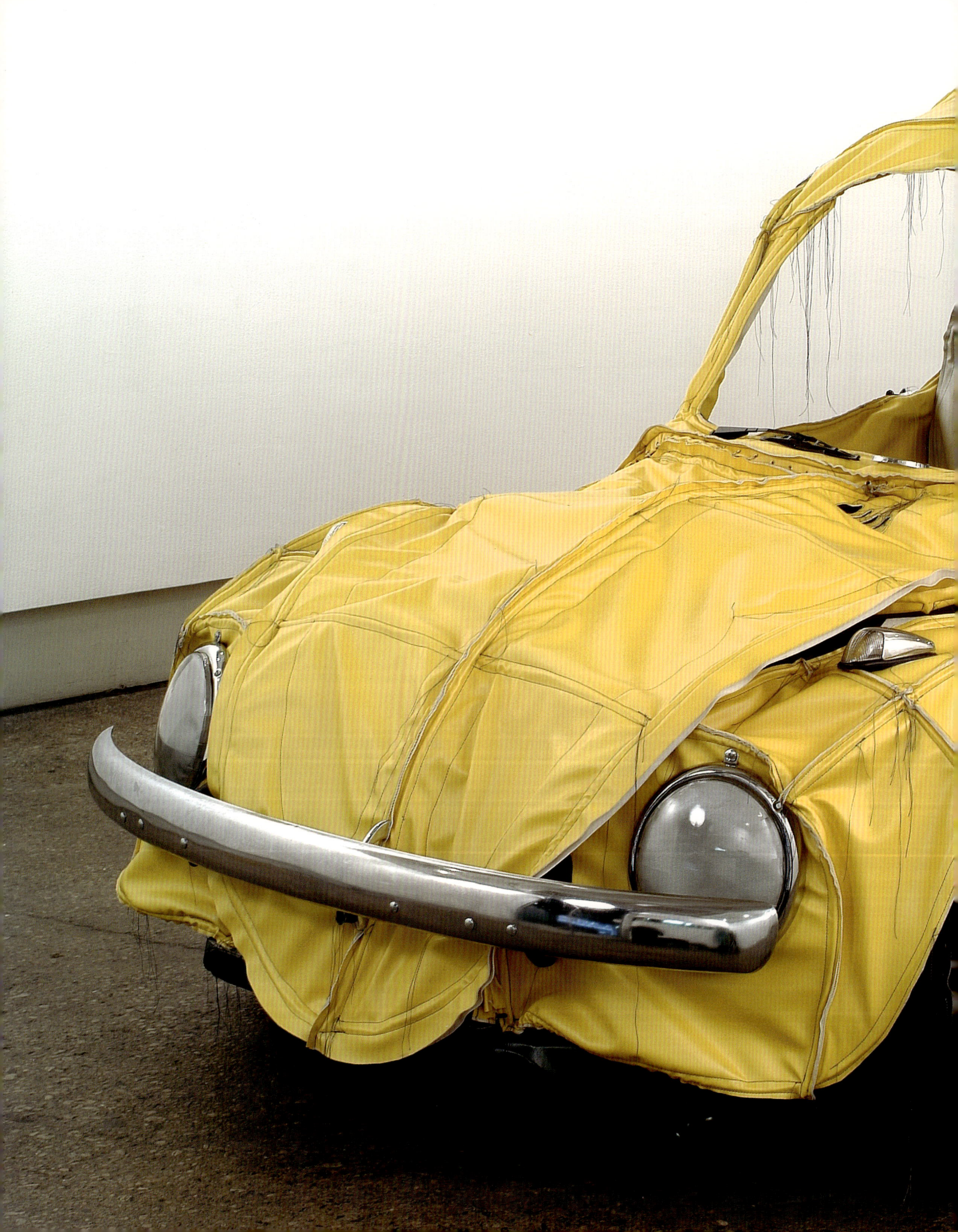

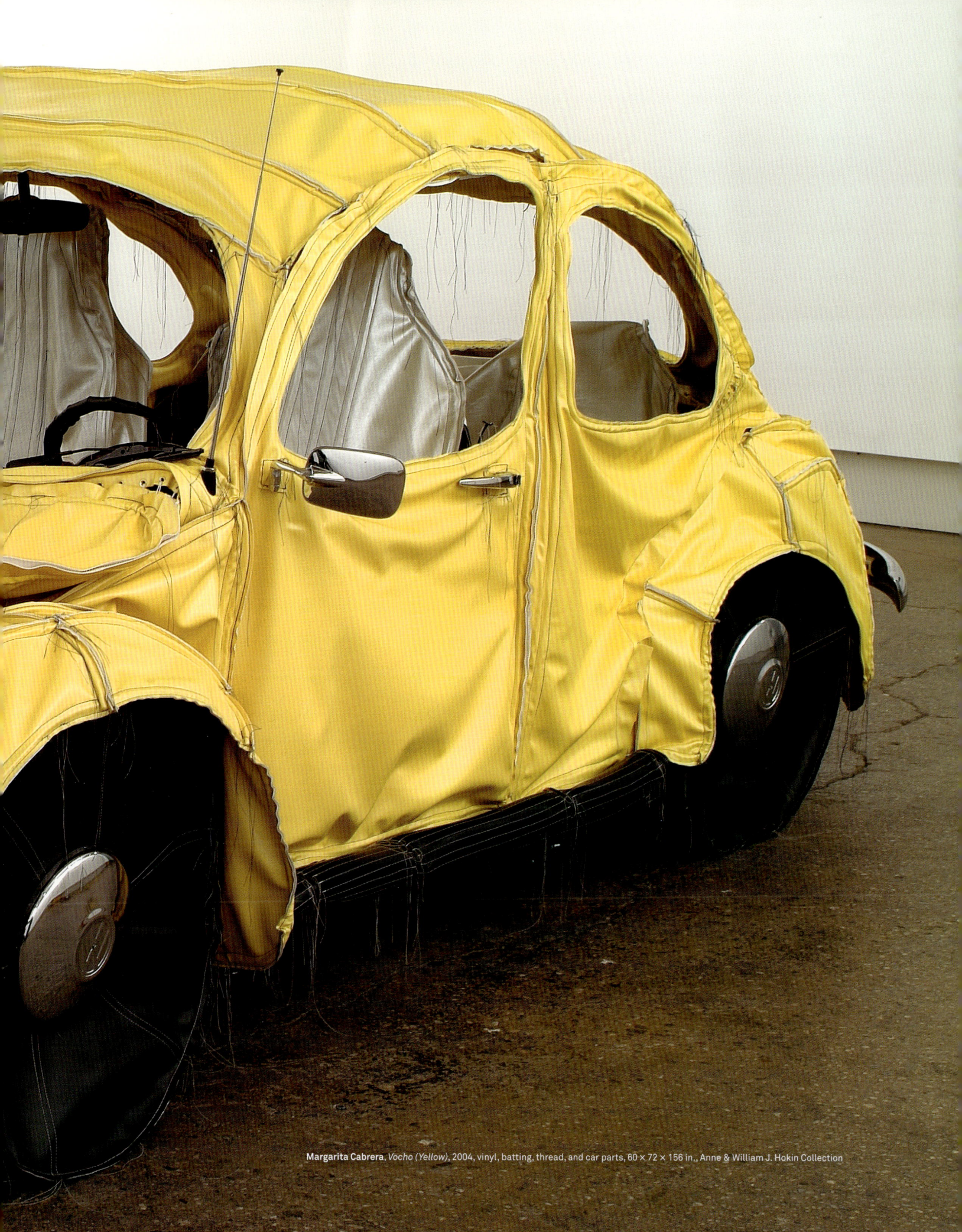

Margarita Cabrera, *Vocho (Yellow)*, 2004, vinyl, batting, thread, and car parts, 60 × 72 × 156 in., Anne & William J. Hokin Collection

today the full complement of his excessive enterprise seems not only inevitable but uniquely generative in our time."[21] Perhaps even more so today, we have to remind ourselves of the radicalism of Warhol's undertaking as his conflation of art production and self-promotion has entered the mainstream.

If the 1980s and 1990s still presented opportunities to intervene in the fabric of the image to decode media strategies and modes of address, today such interventions seem patently tied up with an analog image culture. The question is, where are the points of departure or collapse today?

One notable development in the first decade of the millennium is a renewed interest in objects and processes. Margarita Cabrera's soft sculptures of 2003–4 measure the geography of labor in a global marketplace. Mexico was the last country in which the original Volkswagen Beetle was produced. A pop culture icon in itself, the car eventually became a victim of technological and aesthetic obsolescence, and in 2003 the last model rolled off the assembly line.[22] As a response, Cabrera reconstructed a Beetle to scale and fashioned every part that was made and assembled in Mexico in vinyl. Sagging like an Oldenburg soft sculpture, it is a ponderous tribute. With a shift from an assembly-line construction of parts to a unique, handmade craft object, Cabrera succinctly emphasizes the work process itself. With *Vocho (Yellow)* (pp. 24–25), the obsolescence and disappearance of a consumer good, and possible implications for local employment, are mapped on a single object.

Classic pop art had borrowed from comics, advertisements, and the supermarket display, in part because their candy-colored vision of happy consumerism could be translated into painting and sculpture to examine artistic and cultural values. Following several decades when abstraction had dominated the artistic discourse, the return to "realism" was suspect in itself. What made this shift even less palatable was that the pop artists of the 1960s imitated or appropriated reproductive techniques from commercial industries. And with this embrace, the artists challenged the very foundation of artistic originality. By contrast, artists in the 1980s and early 1990s singled out the photographic image for scrutiny. The construction of image narratives that informed and framed mainstream notions of identity, that propagated stereotypical role models, were the key targets in the 1980s and early 1990s. The subtle implications of hierarchies, gender identities, and subliminal messages were critically examined as constructs. Under a scrutinizing gaze, image culture was recognized as a socially and politically coded minefield, and artists' maneuvers within the visual fabric of images and texts provided rich opportunities for conceptual critiques.

The strategies as well as the assumptions driving these queries are givens for artists working today. And with the accelerated distribution of advertising and consumer goods through the Internet, marketing campaigns have become more individualized and targeted but have also migrated or expanded from public spaces to any number of electronic devices. For a meaningful engagement with commodity culture

21. Jack Bankowsky, "Pop Life," in *Pop Life: Art in a Material World*, exhibition catalogue edited by Jack Bankowsky, Alison M. Gingeras, and Catherine Wood (London: Tate Publishing, 2009), 20.
22. A retooled Beetle, sleeker in design and with more comfortable amenities, was introduced in 1998 and updated in 2011; both versions appeal to younger generations, as well as those nostalgic for the original car.

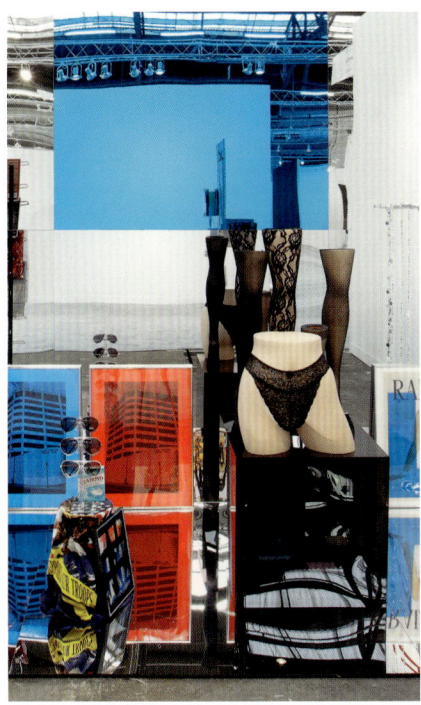

Josephine Meckseper, *American Mall* (detail), 2010, mixed media, 120 × 282 × 48 in., courtesy of Andrea Rosen Gallery, New York

today, artists such as Josephine Meckseper, Elad Lassry, and Rachel Harrison use different strategies. Much of their work centers on the aesthetics of product display. A strange paradox hinges on the display today. In physical manifestation, as arrangements of merchandise in store windows or interiors, such displays are losing ground. At the same time, the demand for product display photography, enhanced by digital editing tools, is soaring. At a time when shoppers spend seconds on the assessment of a particular good in those carefully crafted online images, these contemporary artists create works that require time and reveal themselves gradually. In other words, their work has an experiential quality that intensifies during the viewing process. Meckseper's *American Mall* (pp. 27, 56, and 84–85), for instance, addresses itself to the viewer as a massive window display riddled with strangeness. It is an installation of oddly paired objects on a polished mirror chessboard that borrows its crystal aesthetics from the showrooms of car dealerships. "The mall," to Meckseper, "has become the ultimate American landscape. It is the modern epicenter of artificial leisure and activity, a new church and museum at once. Everything is on display: commodities, entertainment, military recruiting, and exploitation of the work force."[23] Meckseper recognizes that she singles out the mall display at a moment of crisis, if not imminent obsolescence. With a staggering number of transactions now conducted over the web, the mall as a place of commerce, entertainment, and socialization is waning. Yet in reaction to the wars fought in Iraq and Afghanistan, Meckseper observes how patriotism and economic interests are interwoven in the language of display. Accordingly, the artist's unlikely object pairings unpack the intertwining of politics, economics, and consumer culture. Cast in patriotic red, white, and blue, the goods and images in Meckseper's display vary from mannequin fragments displaying hosiery and stockings, to images of race cars staged to look like predators, company logos, and armatures for product display, which are punctured by geometric-style paintings, magazine racks, a tribute to American troops, beads, scrubbing pads, and insignia of power: a medley you wouldn't find in any single shop window. The unifying element is an aesthetic of metallic sheen bathed in cold white light that renders endless surface reflections. The inner ruptures drive home the point that economy and politics, consumption and foreign intervention go hand in hand. To the artist, these works are, "in a sense, time capsules for a near and far future. They represent everything that is wrong with our culture and a possible end phase of an expanding global capitalism that may or may not be sustainable in a few decades. They are dubious souvenirs of our time."[24] Not surprisingly, Meckseper's display includes several abstract paintings by her hand next to the mass-produced goods that rhetorically situate the art product as a consumer article like any other mall object.

Arguably, the critiques of representation that were alive and well in the 1980s and early 1990s have all but exhausted themselves. Much of the appropriation work of that period appealed to viewers at a conceptual level: by isolating, reproducing, and reframing visual

23. Josephine Meckseper, "Interview with Francesco Bonami," in *Josephine Meckseper* (New York: The Flag Art Foundation, 2011), 5.
24. Ibid.

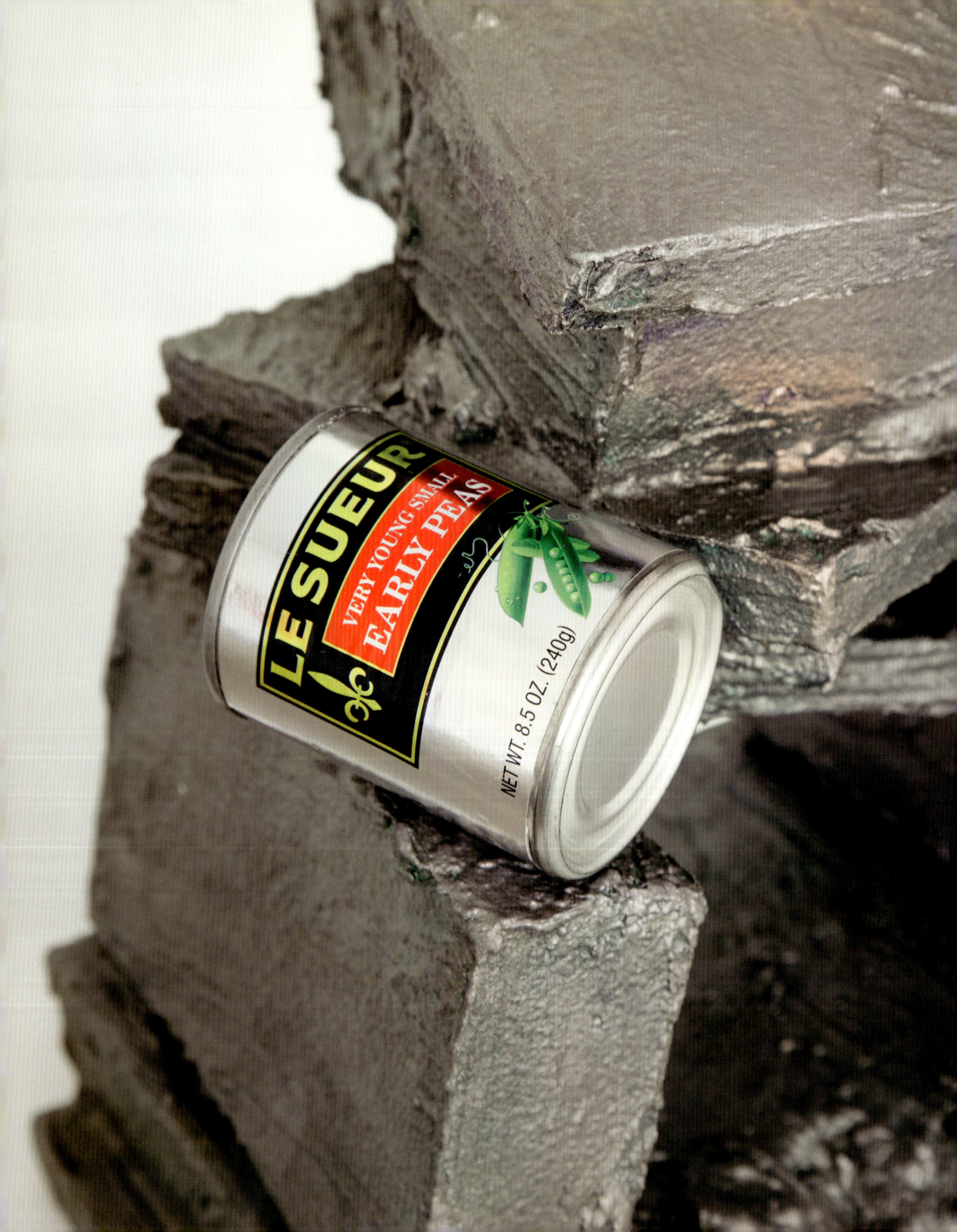

Rachel Harrison, *Very Young Small* (detail), 2005, cast resin, acrylic, and peas, 16¾ × 16¼ × 9¼ in., image courtesy of the artist and Greene Naftali, New York

patterns and strategies, its artists presumably hoped to turn all of us into more critical consumers of image culture. This form of address does not translate well into today's culture of participation. In addition, the kind of advertisements that circulated in the public realm at the time —whether on billboards, magazines, or popular television shows—no longer exist in the same way. With changing media platforms and targeted marketing attacks that are based on individual social media and website choices and tracking, the widespread resonance of particular campaigns, such as that featuring the Marlboro man, is hard to imagine in this more compartmentalized market economy. Artists in the 1980s and early 1990s appealed largely to the viewers' intellect. Recently, artists have taken a different approach and introduced visual elements that shatter the happy spectacle of the display. They stage a subtle discomfort that registers first on an emotive level and subsequently triggers an analytical response.

Elad Lassry's photographic objects are as confounding as Josephine Meckseper's installations. His staged images mine the language of commercial displays, but despite the high image resolution and crisp colors of his photographs there is an air of outdatedness that borders on camp. Just as in Meckseper's work, the viewer trips over an aesthetic construct that is shot through with inconsistencies. Modest in scale, Lassry's painted frames match a dominant color in the photograph and become a design element that extends the carefully arranged image composition. Their can't-quite-place-it strangeness stems from combinations that don't fit our expectations: Green plastic spoons and paper napkins are arranged along with several pieces of cheese on a cold, shiny table (pp. 22 and 87). Neither the clinical shine of the table nor the light-green backdrop showcases the items on display in an especially appetizing fashion. Similarly puzzling are four painted eggs on pastel-colored mini pedestals that might be more suitable for the display of cosmetics (p. 87). *Portrait, Purple* (p. 86) looks like an appropriated yearbook photograph from the 1970s but is actually painstakingly recreated with a contemporary male model. Lassry's displays revisit painting, graphic design, product display, animal photography, and portraiture and borrow from the stylistic vocabulary of magazines, model agency photography, and yearbook pictures. This spirit of reenactment, in contrast to 1980s-style image appropriation, was singled out by the writer and curator Tim Griffin, who argued it signaled "a new importance and ambiguity for notions of immediacy versus mediation in art making, effectively making the matter of representation into one of re-presentation."[25] If appropriation is an exact copy of an image or object that has a circulation and history within popular culture, the reenactment or restaging—as in both Meckseper's and Lassry's work —is a distinctively different undertaking. Today, online commerce nearly collapses the distinction between image and product, since the image is no longer an enticement to visit a store but the decisive factor in purchasing an item. With this shift, the seduction of the image and the compelling presentation of a product is perhaps more crucial for retailers than ever before. By contrast, reenactment allows artists to

25. Tim Griffin, "Coming to Life," in *Elad Lassry: 2000 Words* (Athens: DESTE Foundation for Contemporary Art, 2013), 9.

inhabit, occupy, and intervene within given structures and models while simultaneously drawing our attention to the aesthetics of display. In an interesting twist, the reenactment becomes noticeable in part because of a hyperperfection that renders surfaces into clinically cold and uninviting arrangements, which get our attention because they repel rather than seduce.

This is a sharp contrast to the strategies that Warhol honed in the 1960s and expanded in the coming decades: he glamourized the object and turned pop stars as much as consumer goods into unforgettable icons. Warhol drew on the lessons learned from working in the advertising industry when consumerism itself was cast as glamorous—a vehicle for envisioning oneself as successful, thriving, and upwardly mobile. Consumerism today is alive and well on a global scale but no longer tinged with that happy optimism. If anything, it is more problematic as younger generations ponder the implications of overconsumption, including the draining of natural resources, the exploitation of labor in developing countries, and the mounting problems of waste and pollution. Appropriately, Lassry is selling us neither products nor glamour. Instead his modestly sized works aim to disrupt our passive consumerism. In his essay on Lassry cited above, Tim Griffin describes how altered roles for mediation—different from the critiques of a mediated image environment so often seen in the 1980s—have become key artistic undertakings since the millennium. Lassry prompts us to look at his images with a probing eye, and it is the perfect execution of a slight aesthetic misalignment that opens the door to a critical analysis of the aesthetics of display under contemporary social and economic realities. Instead of being seduced by the visual arrangements, viewers find themselves in the position of popular culture historians trying to unlock the image code and the multitude of references.

The precarious status of the art object (implicit in Meckseper's work, as well as that of Lassry) is also a question pondered by Rachel Harrison. For more than a decade, she has incorporated consumer items and photographs into her sculptures. *Very Young Small* (pp. 28 and 89) is a lopsided resin structure that is accompanied by a can of green peas. The advertising slogan on the product label lends the work its title. The can of vegetables is meant to be picked up and placed anywhere in, around, or on top of Harrison's resin structure, giving the "sculpture" the status of a prop, pedestal, or backdrop. Harrison uses cast resin and acrylic, which has the visual appeal and tactile quality of faux environments in zoos or outdoor entertainment parks. The material is shaped and painted to approximate something else—in this instance it suggests a pile of bricks or building materials. This association is undercut by a color and lumpy texture that is obviously synthetic. Tate curator Catherine Wood rightly points out that Harrison's work is all about display, alluding both to art displays and shop window displays but precisely without the seduction that would entice you to want to own the object. If the can of peas is at least vaguely appealing, the resin structure is unattractive to the point of ugliness and all but teeters near collapse. The contrast between the designed label of the canned

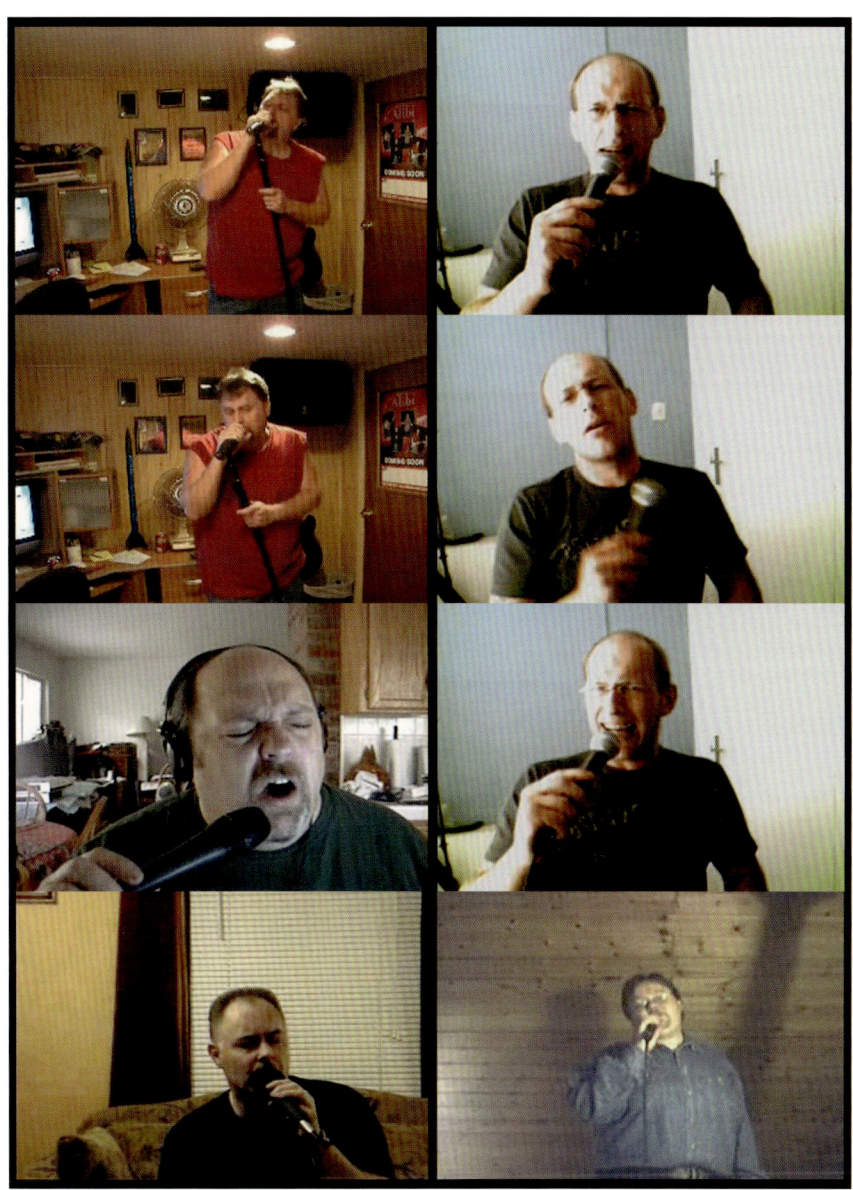

Amie Siegel, *My Way 2* (stills compilation), 2009, video, 12 min., courtesy of Simon Preston Gallery, New York

good—which self-consciously refers back to Andy Warhol's famous Campbell's soup cans—and the cheap, disheveled-looking "sculpture" serves a particular purpose. As Wood puts it, "Harrison recognizes and represents a repressed terror regarding the true nature of those overproduced things we obsessively acquire and surround ourselves with, a recognition from which the art object is not excluded."[26] Harrison's shoddy-looking sculptures are the opposite—low tech, ramshackle, and seemingly cheap, they have a certain built-in resistance that enables them to pose the question of their precarious status as art object and consumer good. Perpetually on display, the promise of the sculpture's title lingers uncomfortably as the work enters the marketplace of art.

As consumer markets migrated to the Internet, so did platforms for self-promotion. This may be one of the most interesting developments since the millennium—Facebook, YouTube, Instagram, Twitter, and related sites keep proliferating at an accelerated speed creating ever-new opportunities to post or share information. In television, film, publishing, and the recording industry, middlemen are disappearing or under duress while any and every individual with a product or talent can broadcast it to the world at large. Warhol may have been overly optimistic in his assessment that in the future everyone would have fifteen minutes of fame, but nearly everyone is trying, and the desire for celebrity, whether classy or schlocky, has become overwhelmingly mainstream. This trend has developed hand in hand with the merging of commercial and private spheres, resulting in strange hybrids.

A perfect example of such hybrids are the many blogs and Facebook or YouTube postings that might be aimed primarily at an insider group of family and friends but can reach a much wider audience. What are the chances that the posting of an image, a stunt, or a performance will go viral overnight and garner a worldwide following in a few hours? That desire to be heard, to express an emotion or desire, is where Amie Siegel's video pair *My Way 1* (p. 95) and *My Way 2* (pp. 31 and 94) hit a nerve. These are compilations of YouTube videos showing individuals performing popular songs in their bedrooms, dens, garages, and attics. *My Way 1* is a compilation of young women singing "Gotta Go My Own Way" from *High School Musical 2* (2007). *My Way 2* gathers video clips posted by men across a diverse age range interpreting Frank Sinatra's "My Way," originally released in 1969. The result is mesmerizing: each performance provides a glimpse into a private universe. Why were the videos—ranging from melancholic to triumphant to camp—recorded? Why are they posted publically? We could be looking at friends goofing off, relationships breaking up, or recordings for talent scouts. Siegel's compilations deliver a compelling slice of contemporary visual culture as the performers channel their dreams and desires. The tacit understanding that exhibitionism and voyeurism are part and parcel of this venture in which the private is voluntarily rendered public has become another commonplace for a generation of networked participants for whom the division of public and private spheres has become fluid or entirely irrelevant.

26. Catherine Wood, "The Stuff: Rachel Harrison's Sculpture," *Afterall: A Journal of Art, Context, and Enquiry*, 11 (Spring/Summer 2005), 42.

Similarly enthralled with the phenomenon of self-production is Ryan Trecartin, whose high-octane videos stage an unlikely cast of characters in endless auditioning and rehearsal scenarios. The format may be best described as a mash-up of Warhol Factory, *Saturday Night Live* skit, reality TV, and blog posting. With makeup and outfits in various stages of decomposition, the interactions center on "communication" —or rather, an endless array of teenage-inflected pronouncements that are pure affect, with each individual focused on prolonged monologues and declarations. Superlatives and emotional self-indulgence is the cacophonous modus operandi that swallows up the rare insightful remark within the torrent. In *Comma Boat* (pp. 92–93), a group of aspirants is directed to rehearse a routine over and over again, without any notable progress. Holed up in a single location, the performers project an empty void lurking behind the melodrama of the exchanges. *Comma Boat* reads like a speed-induced version of *Waiting for Godot* for generation Y. The ever-present handheld camera serves as a reminder that in this alternate universe the only reality of consequence is on-screen, with the final cut or finished routine never in sight.

The foregrounding of a culture of display—whether in the staging of objects or individuals—is emerging as an important arena in which artists today are exercising their critical thinking. Rather than the conceptual appeals to the intellect in 1980s-style photo-conceptual appropriations, these recent works appeal first to our gut. The tinge of strangeness, surrealness, or discomfort that is built into their fabric prompts us to look harder and becomes the key to a broader critique of this brave new world of self-production, display, and consumption where appearance and presentation tend to outweigh self-reflection and thought.

THE FIRST POP AGE: TWO EXCERPTS

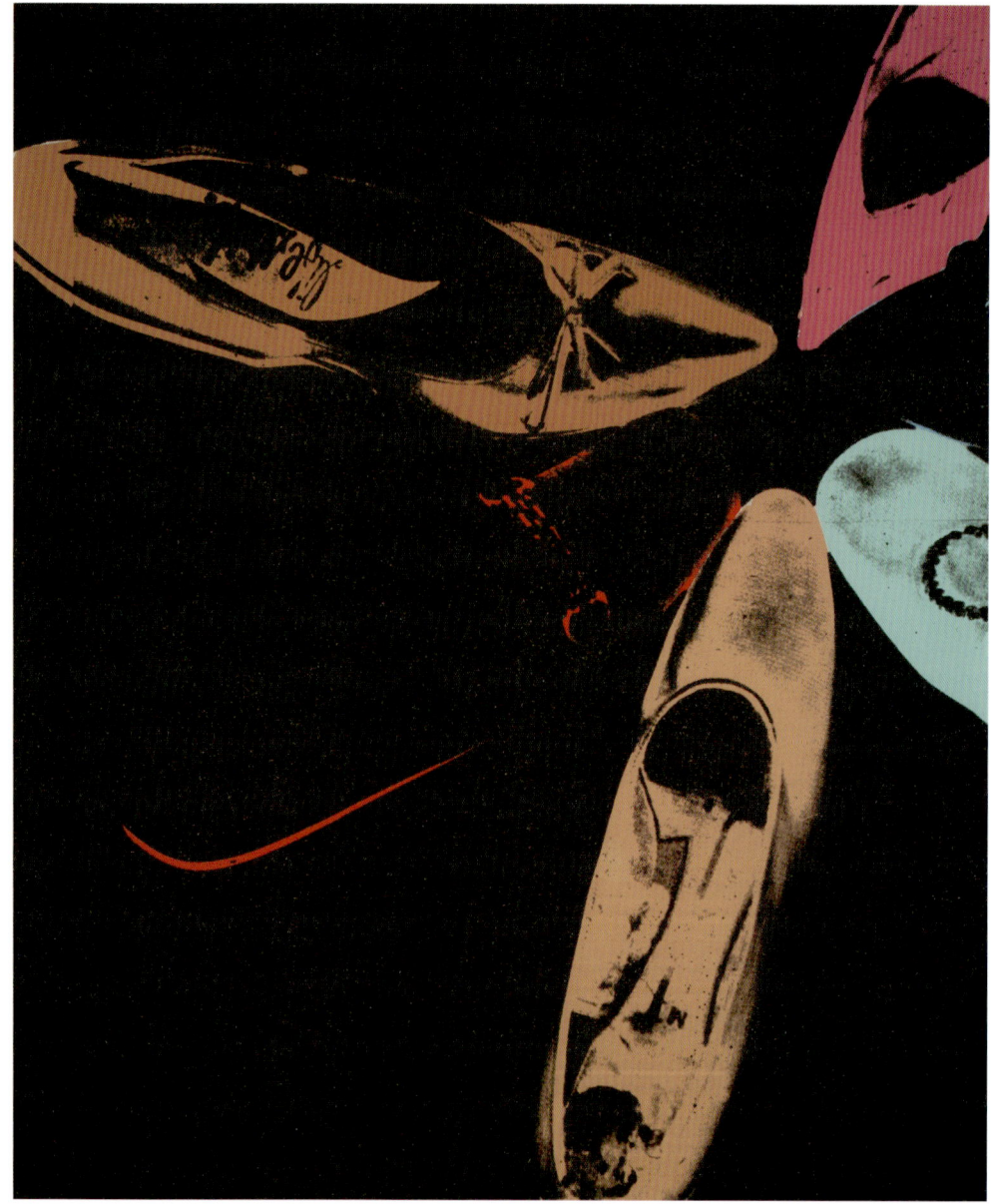

Andy Warhol, *Diamond Dust Shoes*, 1980–81,
acrylic, silkscreen ink, and diamond dust on linen, 49¾ × 42 in., Janet Ketcham Collection

HAL FOSTER
CRITIC

THE FIRST POP AGE: TWO EXCERPTS

Like much literature and criticism of the time (the first novels of J.G. Ballard, for example), Pop proposed that subjectivity had surfaced into the world, with the psychological interiorities of bourgeois selfhood now confused with the everyday exteriorities of consumerist life. For all its emphasis on surfaces, however, Pop still registers the subjective (even, I argue, the traumatic), and perhaps nowhere more so than in its manifold moves to *suspend* the subjective: not only in its persistent use of inexpressive gestures and neutral styles, of banal motifs and stupid photos, but also in its mimetic exacerbation of a mass culture calculated to manipulate the subject, which was once understood to be autonomous. As a result, Pop art often suggests paradoxical structures of feeling, looking, and meaning: an affect that is flat one moment and intense the next; a gaze that is deadpan at times and desirous at others; a significance that seems all but absent at first glance and superabundant a second later, with the viewer positioned as a blank scanner one moment and a frenetic iconographer the next.

—

If painting persists in Pop, then, so do the pressures of modern life. It is for this reason that I draw on concepts proposed long ago to describe the effects of this modernity, concepts like "reification," "fetishization," and "distraction." As they appear in Pop, these effects are heightened by the technological advances of modernity in the postwar period, and in its mimesis, Pop makes them even more emphatic. Thus Pop shows us how, in a consumerist economy, objects and images tend to become serial and simulacral, and how commodities tend to operate like signs and vice versa. Indeed, Pop works to capture a shift in appearance whereby the commercial world appears as a second nature shot through with photographic, filmic, and televisual visualities. In this condition, reification, which once described the routine objectification of human relations in capitalist production and consumption, comes to look like its apparent opposite, that is to say, less a becoming thing-like than a becoming liquid or light, as though what Karl Marx and Friedrich Engels had only imagined in *The Communist Manifesto* (1848) about the capitalist dynamic at large—"all that is solid melts into air"—had actually come to pass. As Pop attempts to paint this changed semblance (which [Richard] Hamilton once described as photographic "phloo," and [Ed] Ruscha as "celluloid gloss"), it sometimes makes this appearance more seductive than it is; Pop does so out of sheer delight, to be sure, but its demonstration has cognitive value too. For in its representation of this glossy world, Pop exposes a general drive not only to pictorialize everything but also to fetishize the images that result, that is, to invest them with a powerful life of their own. Such is the theory of consumer capitalism that Pop implies: its political economy depends on a compounding of sexual, commodity, and semiotic fetishisms, a "super-fetishism" in which the making of products, images, and signs becomes evermore obscure while our investment in these phantoms becomes evermore intense.

—

Hal Foster, *The First Pop Age: Painting and Subjectivity in the Art of Hamilton, Lichtenstein, Warhol, Richter, and Ruscha* (Princeton, NJ: Princeton University Press, 2012), 7–8 and 12–13. Used by permission of the author.

36

WARHOL AND AFTER

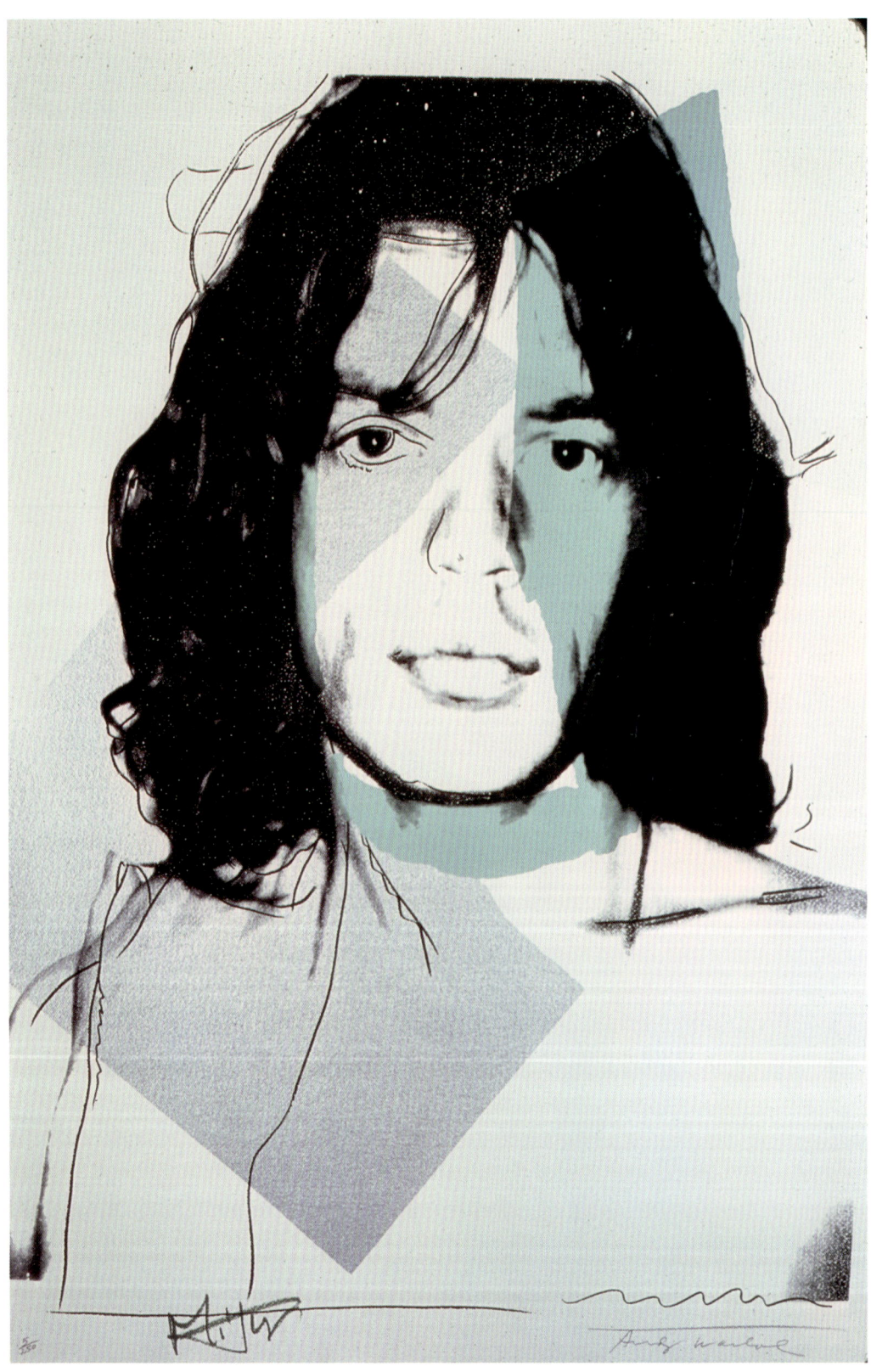

Andy Warhol, *Mick Jagger (#1)*, 1975, screenprint on Arches Aquarelle paper, 44 × 29¼ in., Seattle Art Museum, Gift of the American Art Foundation, 79.88

RICHARD MEYER
ART HISTORIAN

WARHOL AND AFTER

In chapter ten of *The Philosophy of Andy Warhol: From A to B and Back Again*, the artist confides that, "I really like to eat alone. I want to start a chain of restaurants for other people who are like me called ANDYMATS— 'The Restaurant for the Lonely Person.' You get your food and then you take your tray into a booth and watch television."[1]

I was thinking about Warhol's ANDYMATS the other day when I walked into a Coffee Bean and Tea Leaf on Market Street in downtown San Francisco. Everyone in the relatively crowded coffee shop seemed to be on his or her own. This is not to say, however, that they were alone. Each patron was tapping away on an iPad, laptop, or cell phone. Partnered with their personal devices, the customers seemed entirely uninterested in (if not outright oblivious to) one another. The café, it seemed to me, had been made over in the image of the ANDYMAT.

Warhol died in 1987, but the legacy of his pop art and cultural sensibility continues to endure, nowhere more so than in the intimate connection that defines our relation to technology. ("When I got my first TV set," Warhol said, "I stopped caring so much about having close relationships."[2]) What need, we might ask after Warhol, for intersubjective relationships to other people when the interaction between self and screen has become so satisfying?

Beyond his self-declared intimacy with his television set and tape recorder (the latter of which the artist called his "wife"), Warhol also remains influential because his work stemmed from a genuine interest in popular and commercial culture rather than a sense of superiority to or ironic remove from it. The artist memorably put the point this way: "The Pop artists did images that anybody walking down Broadway could recognize in a split second—comics, picnic tables, men's trousers, celebrities, shower curtains, refrigerators, Coke bottles —all the great modern things that the Abstract Expressionists tried so hard not to notice at all."[3]

What was important to Warhol was not only the "great modern things" that inhabit the commercial landscape of contemporary life—the comics and shower curtains, the celebrities and Coke bottles—but also the way in which a leading group of avant-garde artists sought to separate their art from, and elevate it above, such things. Warhol proposed instead that we embrace the logic of the marketplace and the poetics of consumer culture. For better or worse, contemporary artists continue to learn from and expand upon his example.

---

1. Andy Warhol, *The Philosophy of Andy Warhol: From A to B and Back Again* (New York: Harcourt Brace Jovanovich, 1975), 160.
2. Ibid., 26.
3. Andy Warhol and Pat Hackett, *Popism: The Warhol '60s* (New York: Harcourt Brace Jovanovich, 1980), 3.

HAIR PORTRAIT #20

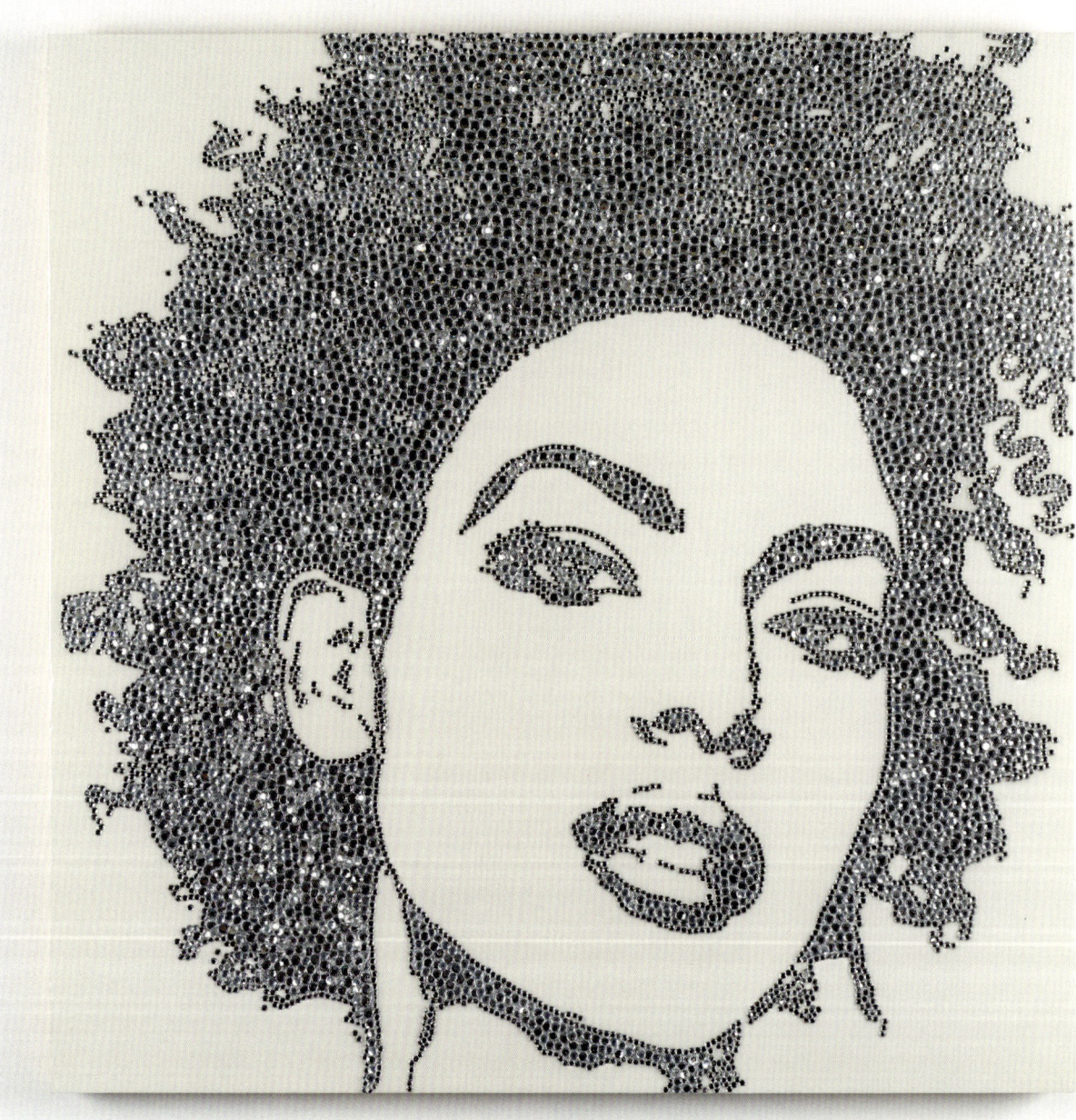

Mickalene Thomas, *Hair Portrait #20* (detail), 2014, plastic rhinestones and acrylic on panel,
30 panels, 30 × 30 in. each, courtesy of the artist and Lehmann Maupin Gallery, New York and Hong Kong

MICKALENE THOMAS
ARTIST

HAIR PORTRAIT #20

My interest in portraiture stems from an ongoing investigation of black female identity and, in particular, the radical potential such ornamental beauty presents in the context of western art history. The black female subject is notably absent from traditional genres of portraiture, and as such, I have been driven by a desire to probe such oversights, question their origin, and augment such notions through a consideration of my own position as an African American woman.

Throughout recent years, I have embarked on an ongoing series of paintings that seeks to document the multitude of diverse, creative, and eccentric approaches to hair styling specific to the African diaspora. My focus is on the multiplicity of forms, patterns, and arrangements through which hair may be threaded—a unique and bold expression of identity and individuality. The subjects of these paintings are often unknown to me; I find inspiration through their expression within the circulation of these images via the worldwide web.

Whereas artists of the first wave of pop art were driven by an interest in spectacle—in celebrity, technology, and the promises afforded through postwar capitalism—my hair portraits entertain a much more modest, though nonetheless significant, possibility. I seek to celebrate and claim moments of beauty and creativity that have otherwise been overlooked through art history, pointing to these quotidian corporeal presentations as significant icons of our time and a crucial element within our cultural landscape.

The means for image production and distribution have been radically democratized through advents in technology (such as digital media), and today consumers have unprecedented agency. Advents in imaging technology mean that the user/consumer simultaneously occupies the role of producer. Such users/consumers/producers are apt to develop a commoditization of their own image, thus rerouting the traditional pathways to both celebrity and commodity.

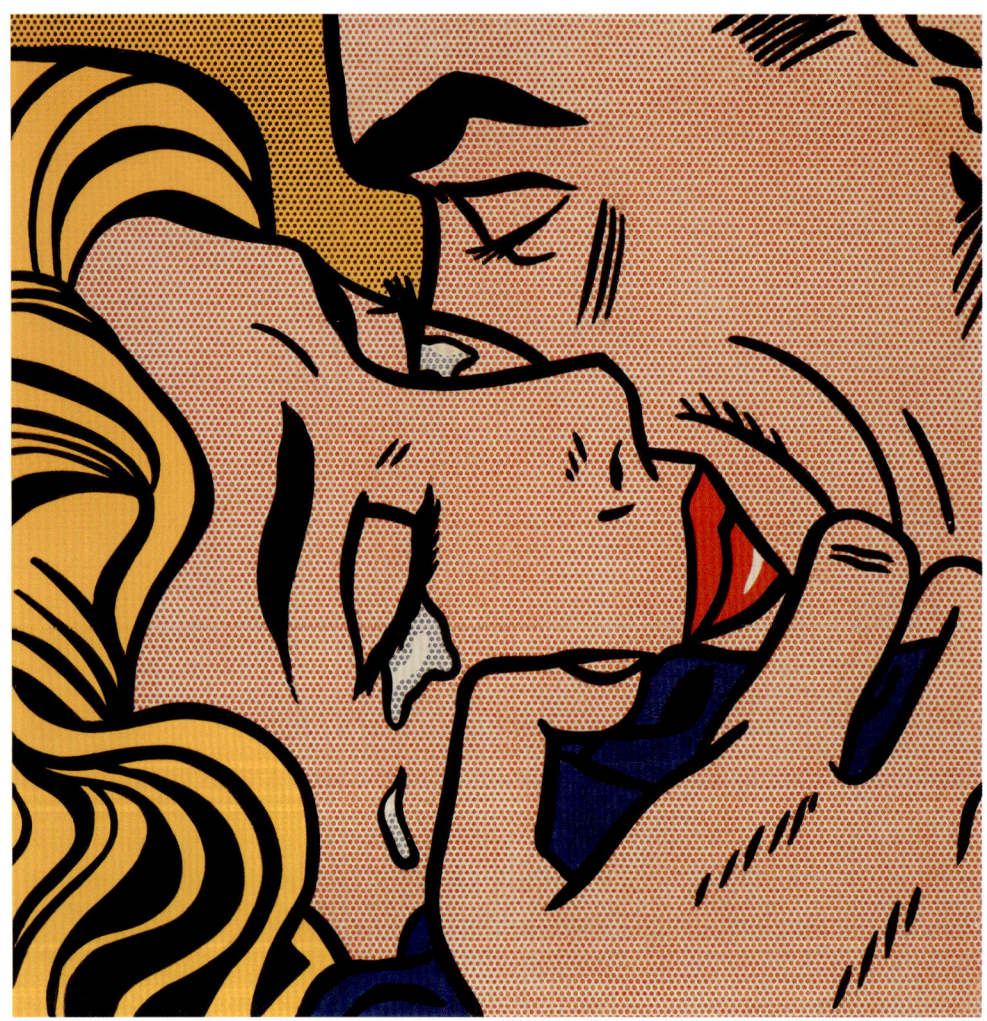

Roy Lichtenstein, *Kiss V*, 1964, magna on canvas, 36 × 36 in., Collection Simonyi

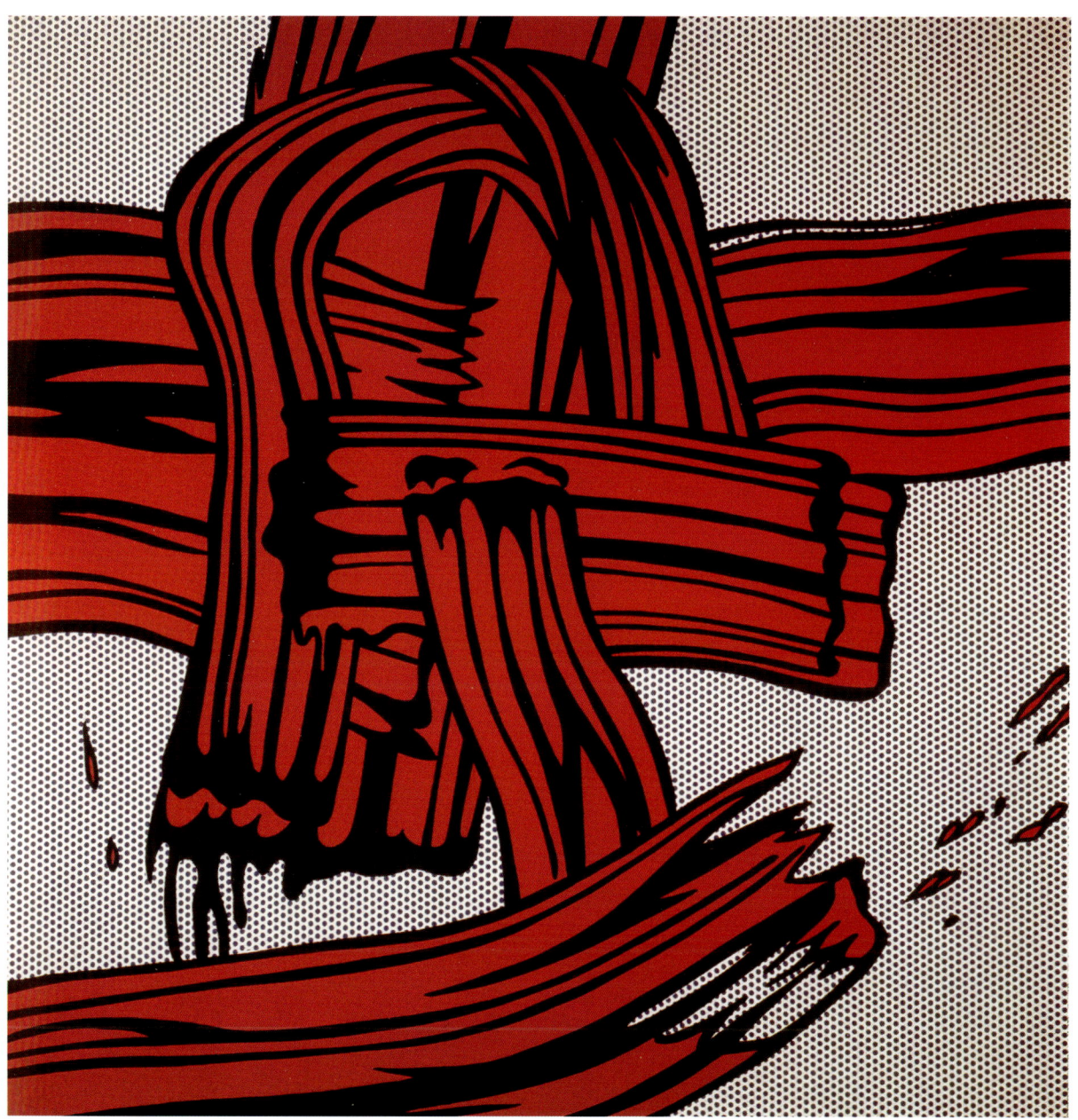

Roy Lichtenstein, *Red Painting (Brushstroke)*, 1965, oil and magna on canvas, 60 × 60 in., Collection Simonyi

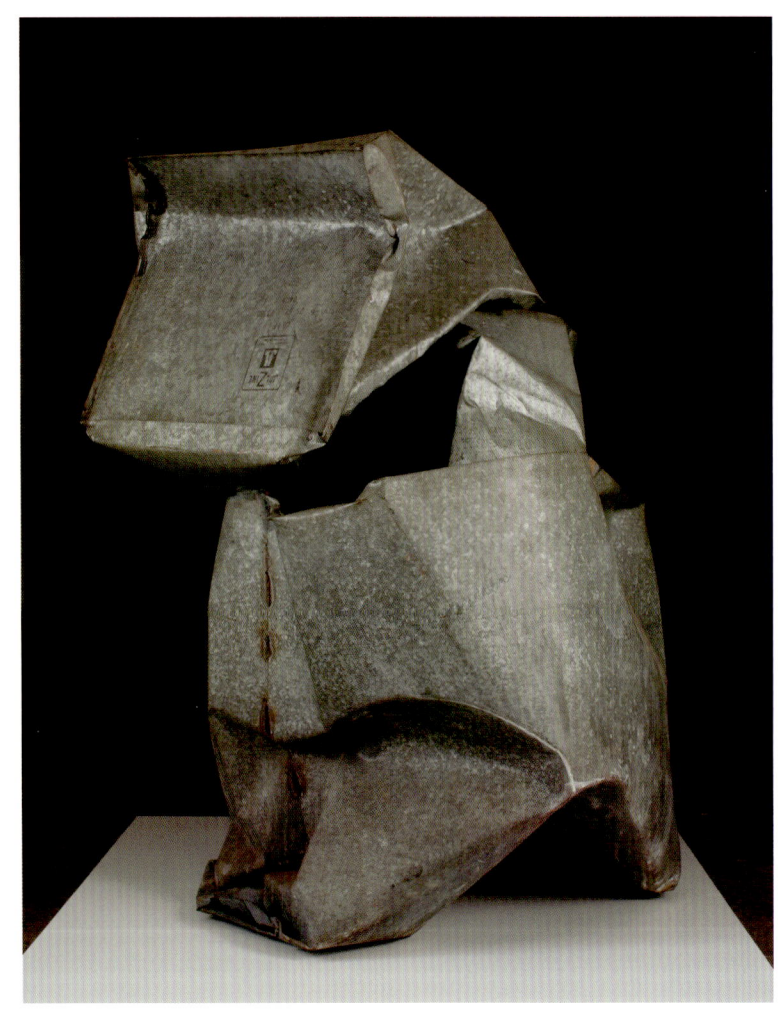

John Chamberlain, *Ultra Yahoo*, 1967, steel, 54 × 59½ × 39 in., private collection

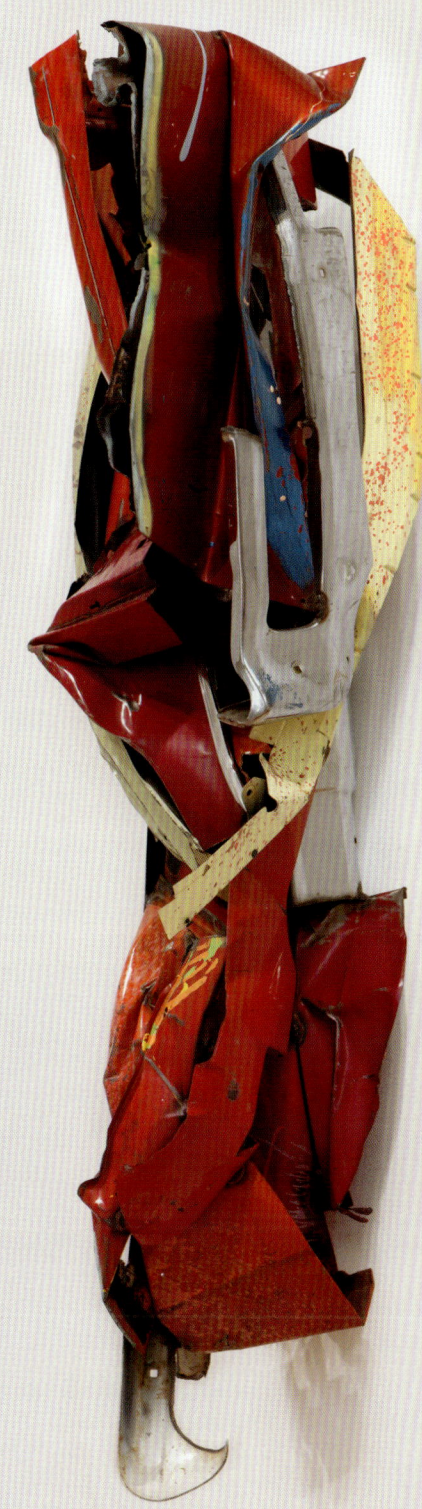

John Chamberlain, *High Tale*, 1978, painted and chrome-painted steel, 84½ × 25 × 32 in., Collection of Jeffrey and Susan Brotman

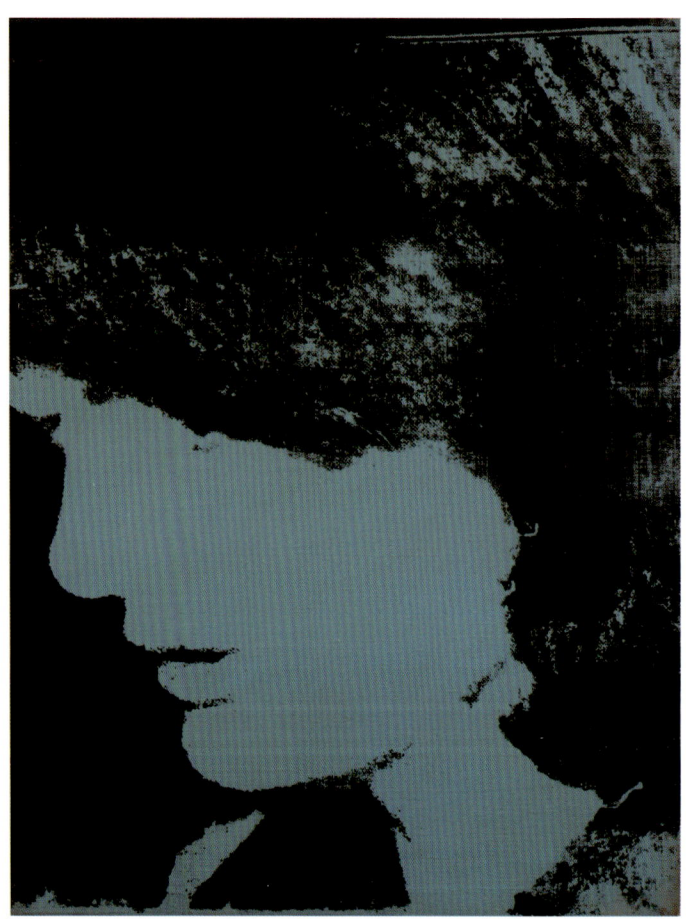

Andy Warhol, *Jackie*, 1964, synthetic polymer paint and silkscreen on canvas, 20 × 16 in., Collection of Jeffrey and Susan Brotman

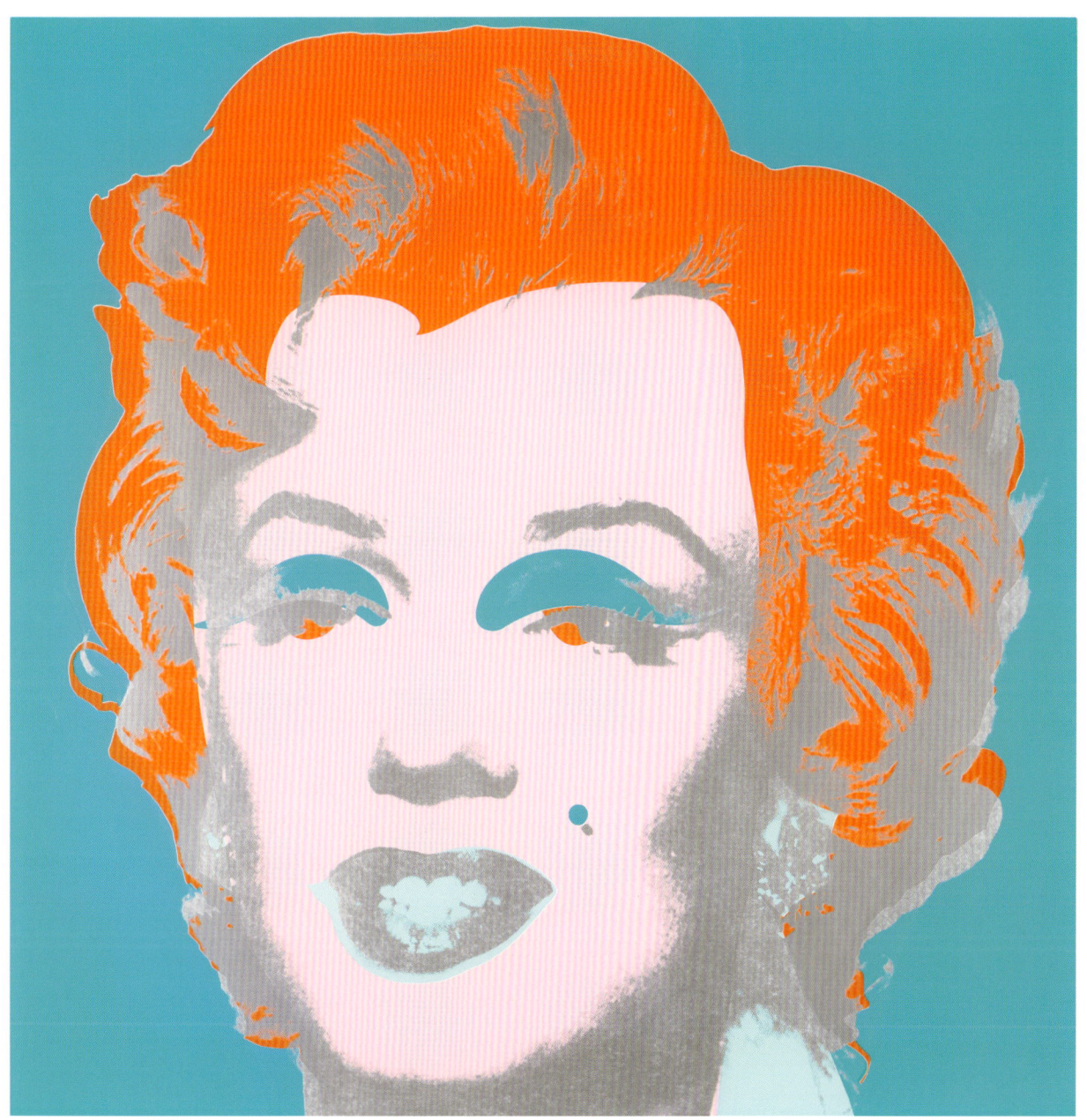

Andy Warhol, *Marilyn*, 1967, screenprint on paper, 36 × 36 in., Seattle Art Museum, Bequest of Kathryn L. Skinner, 2004.119

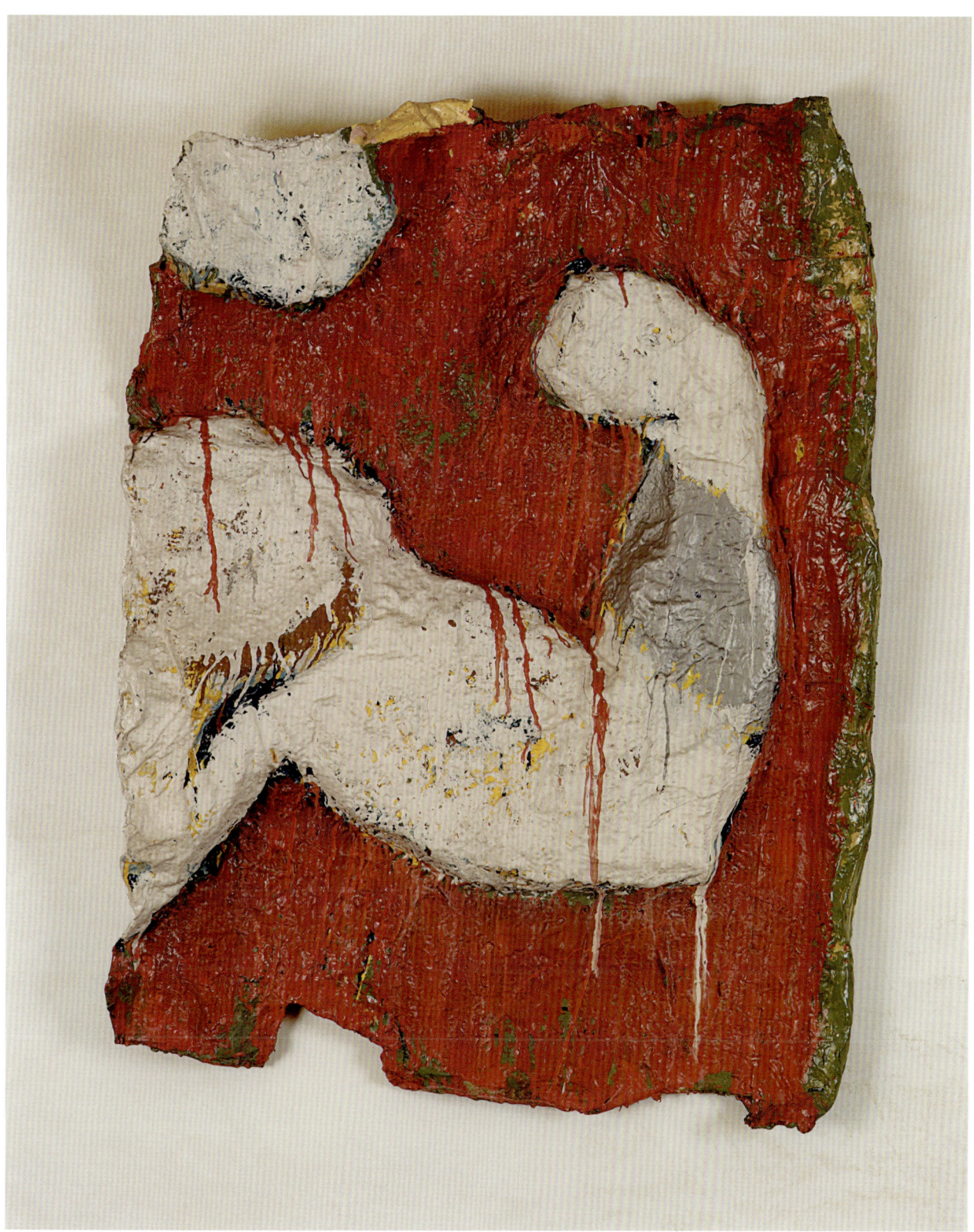

Claes Oldenburg, *Strong Arm*, 1961, plaster and enamel paint, 43 × 42 in., Collection of Barney A. Ebsworth

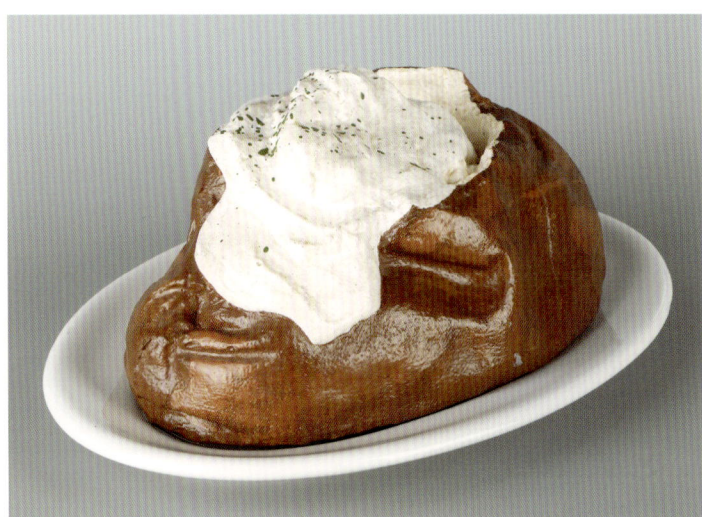

Claes Oldenburg, *Baked Potato*, 1966, cast resin painted with acrylic, Shenango China dish, 4½ × 10½ × 7 in., Seattle Art Museum, Gift of Sidney and Anne Gerber, 86.274.4

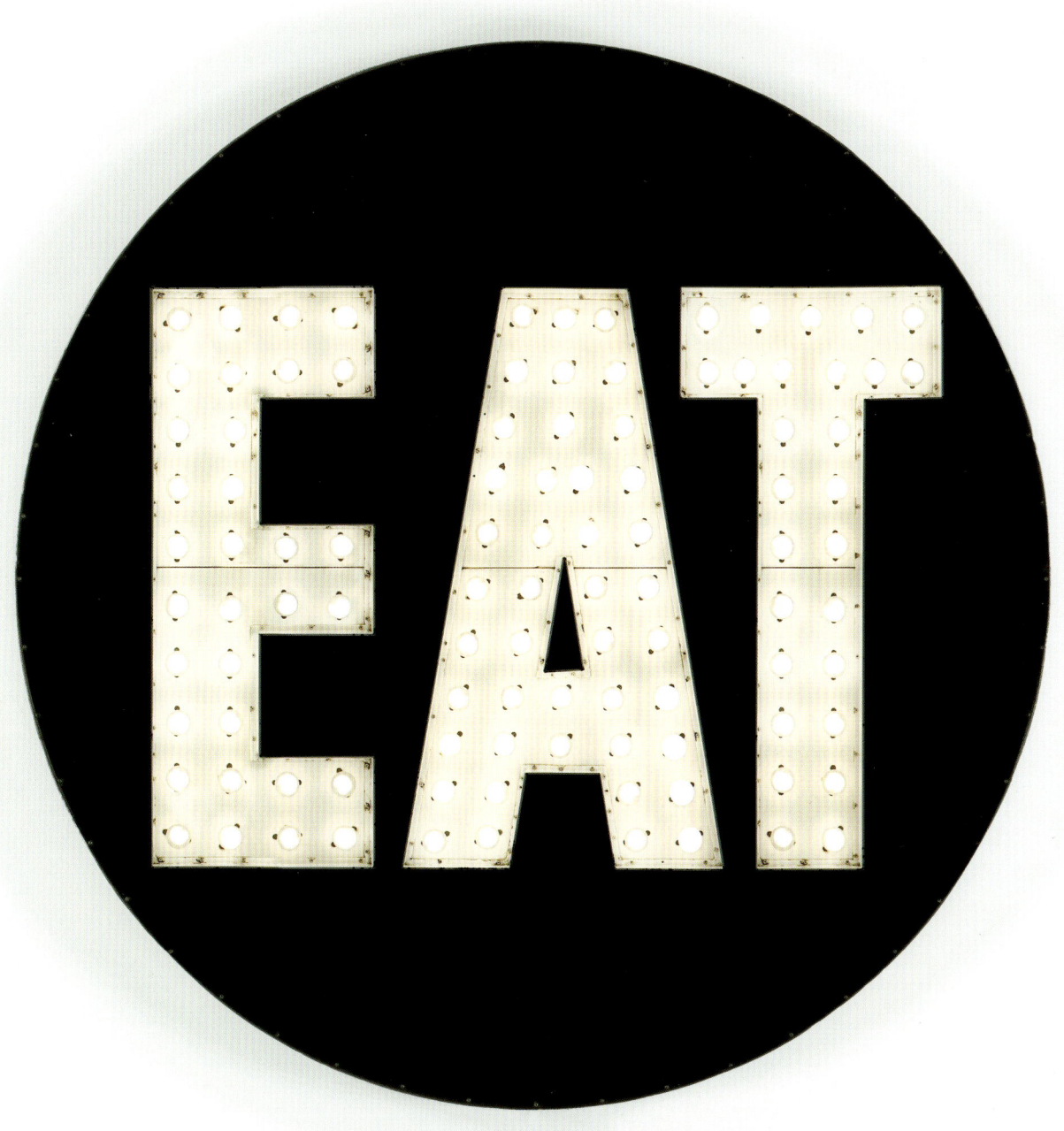

Robert Indiana, *The Electric EAT*, 1964 / 2007, polychrome aluminum, stainless steel, and lightbulbs, 78 × 78 × 7 in., private collection

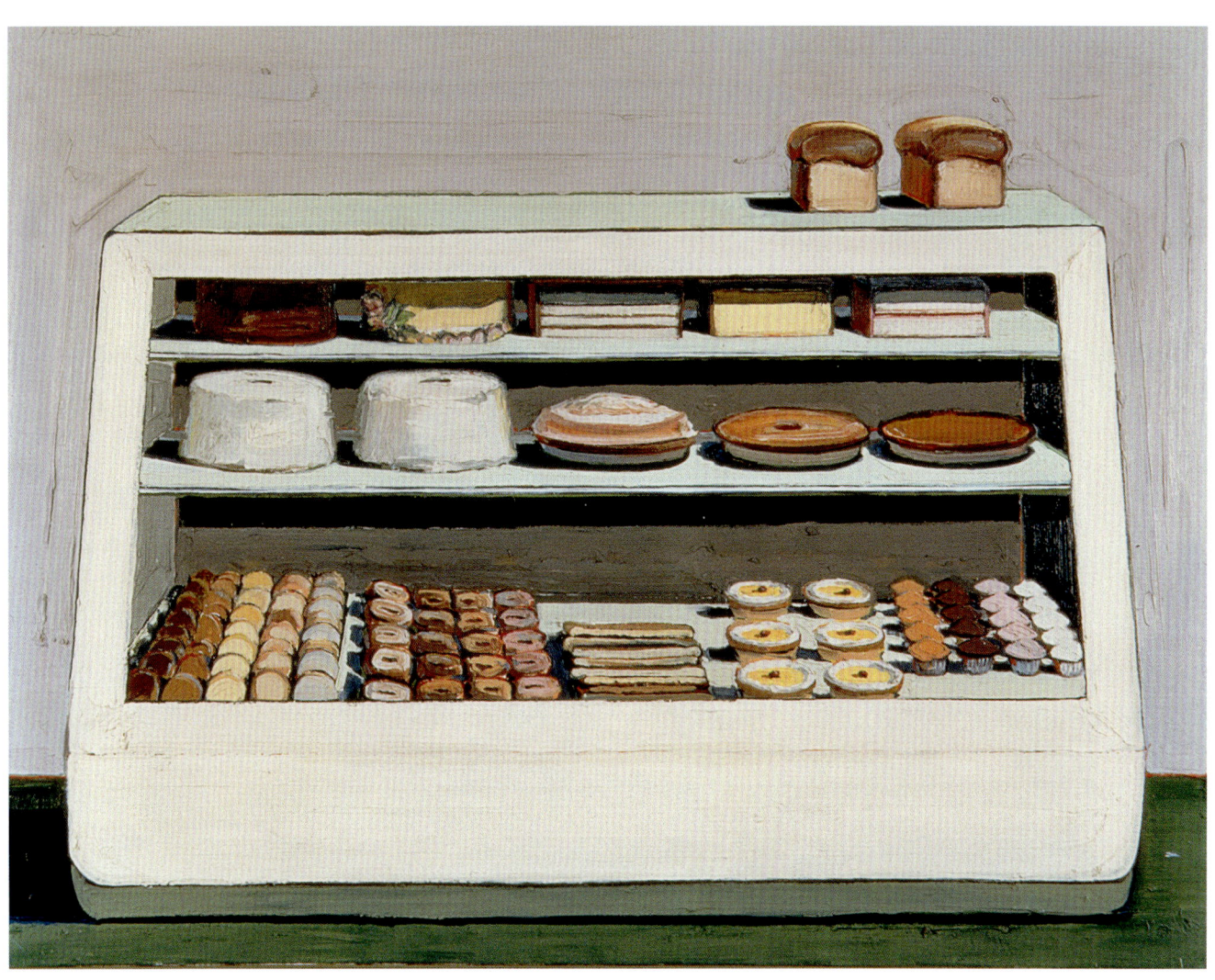

Wayne Thiebaud, *Bakery Counter*, 1962, oil on canvas, 54⅞ × 71⅞ in., Collection of Barney A. Ebsworth, © Wayne Thiebaud / Licensed by VAGA, New York

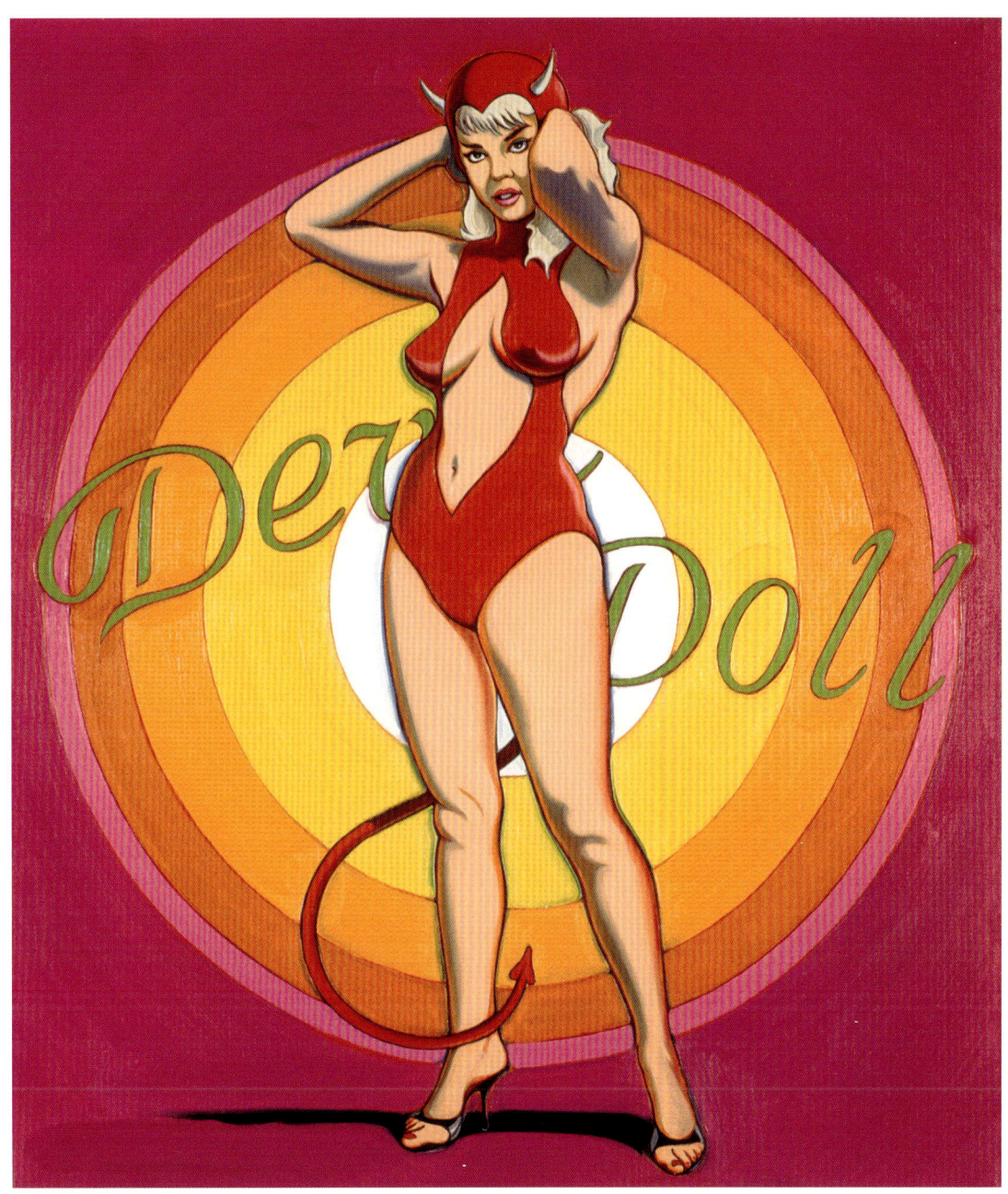

Mel Ramos, *Devil Doll*, 1963–64, oil on canvas, 50 × 44 in., Louis K. Meisel Gallery, © Mel Ramos / Licensed by VAGA, New York

54

PERIOD ROOMS

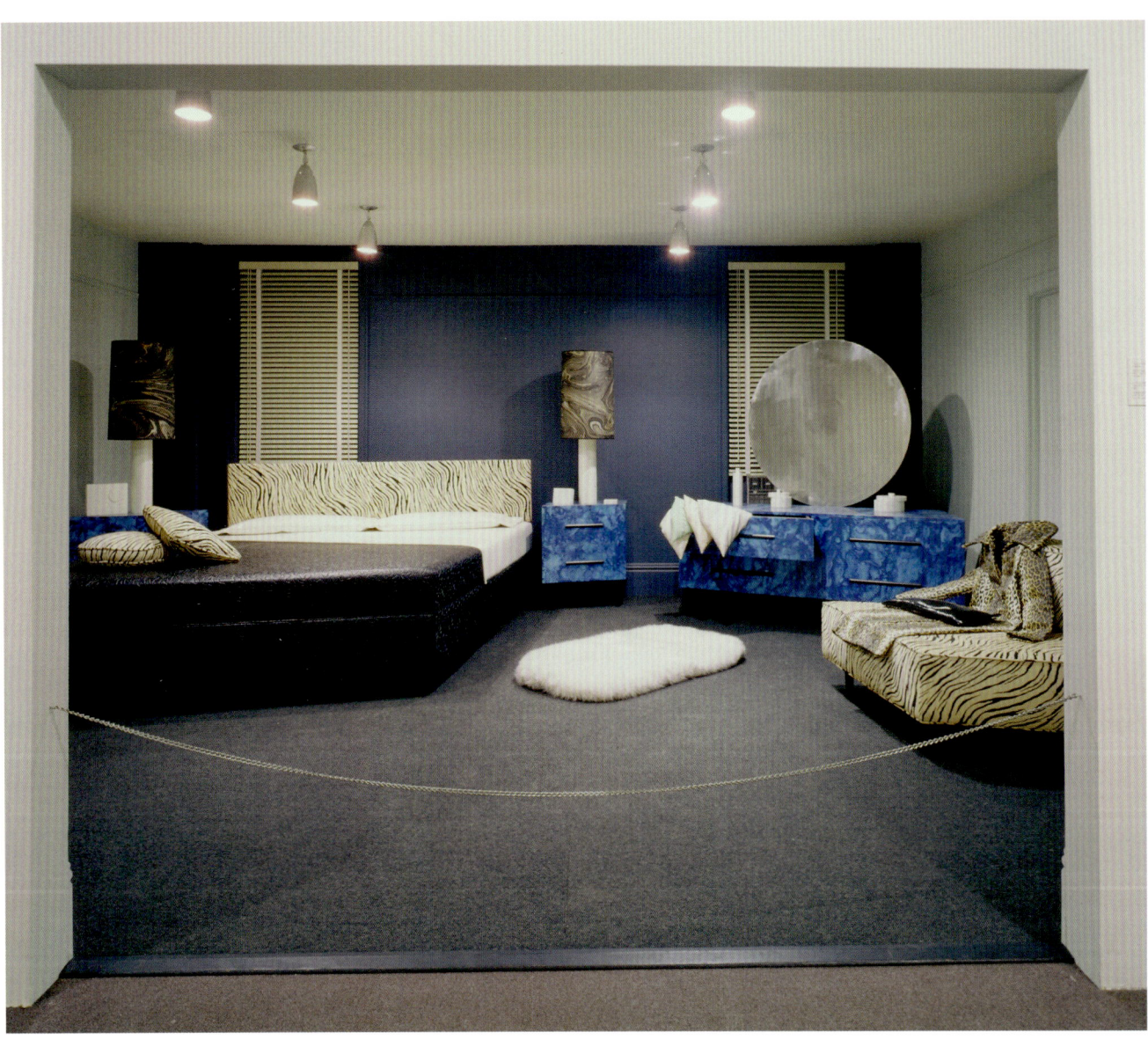

Claes Oldenburg, *Bedroom Ensemble*, 1963, wood, vinyl, metal, artificial fur, cloth, and paper, 118 × 256 × 207 in., National Gallery of Canada, Ottawa

KEN ALLAN
ART HISTORIAN

PERIOD ROOMS

Claes Oldenburg's *Bedroom Ensemble* (1963, opposite page) is a full-scale recreation of a tacky Malibu hotel room with oddly distorted furniture constructed as if it were subject to a photograph's foreshortening. When critic Barbara Rose asked Oldenburg whether the piece was a sculpture, he replied: "Of course it's a sculpture, but I wanted people to feel it with their eyes, so to speak, to stand there and see the whole thing."[1] Oldenburg hints at one of pop's most powerful legacies—the emphasis on new modes of seeing and experience that accompanied the commercial materials and processes of reproduction that artists employed in this work of the 1960s. I sense that "the whole thing" that Oldenburg wants us to see here is more than the work itself, but something about the predicament of American culture that created the desire to inhabit such a false, illusory space complete with a zebra-stripe printed headboard. If our desires, now splintered into myriad niches, have only become more conditioned and easily anticipated by the powers that be since the 1960s, it is striking how contemporary artists such as Josephine Meckseper return our attention to the props and staging of scenes of (visual) consumption.

Meckseper's *American Mall* (2010, pp. 27, 56, and 84–85) is a full-scale environment, but like Oldenburg's bedroom, it is a space oriented primarily to the eye, a tableau that makes palpable the experience of looking. The mirrored floor and back wall create a disorienting profusion of images, surfaces, and reflections and the sculpture becomes a picture composed with the tools of retail (and museum) display. But if the ridiculous period décor of Oldenburg's bedroom allows viewers to laugh at anyone who would actually enjoy such a place and the lifestyle it implies, Meckseper collapses that distance by including us in the work—we are reflected in the mirror among all the items on display.

What is on offer in *American Mall* are not only the easily identifiable consumer items featured in 1960s pop art, but radical books such as *Chomsky on Anarchism*, "Support our Troops" paraphernalia, and a copy of *Artforum* magazine. The cover of this particular issue of *Artforum* features an image of a magazine piece by artist Dan Graham that was published next to a bra advertisement within the pages of *Harper's Bazaar* in 1968. This historical example of an artist's intervention into the discourse of fashion is on display here like everything else, including an actual copy of *Harper's Bazaar* and a pair of women's underwear. A Ralph Lauren ad, to which Meckseper has collaged pieces of blue and red transparent film, is framed like a work of art—so what is the difference between this and Graham's conceptual piece, which was surrounded by ads in a women's magazine, now presented to us in a museum vitrine?

Looking at *American Mall*, we become conscious of the importance of reading these framing devices in order to make distinctions between, or to note the erosion of differences among, the kinds of culture on display here. Meckseper limns the language of visual presentation for us, not unlike the way Oldenburg wanted us to "feel" how his sculpture had already been consumed as an image through its perspectival distortions. Perhaps Meckseper's insistence on materiality in her work—all the racks, plinths, hangers, and stands—is a reminder that the technology of display and the "platforms" of presentation are forms of power even in the digital age when the marketplace —of goods and ideas—is becoming increasingly immaterial and spectacular.

---

1. Claes Oldenburg, interview with Barbara Rose (undated), Barbara Rose Papers, Series II, Box 1, Folder 28, Getty Research Institute, quoted in Judith Rodenbeck, *Radical Prototypes: Allan Kaprow and the Invention of Happenings* (Cambridge: MIT Press, 2011), 58.

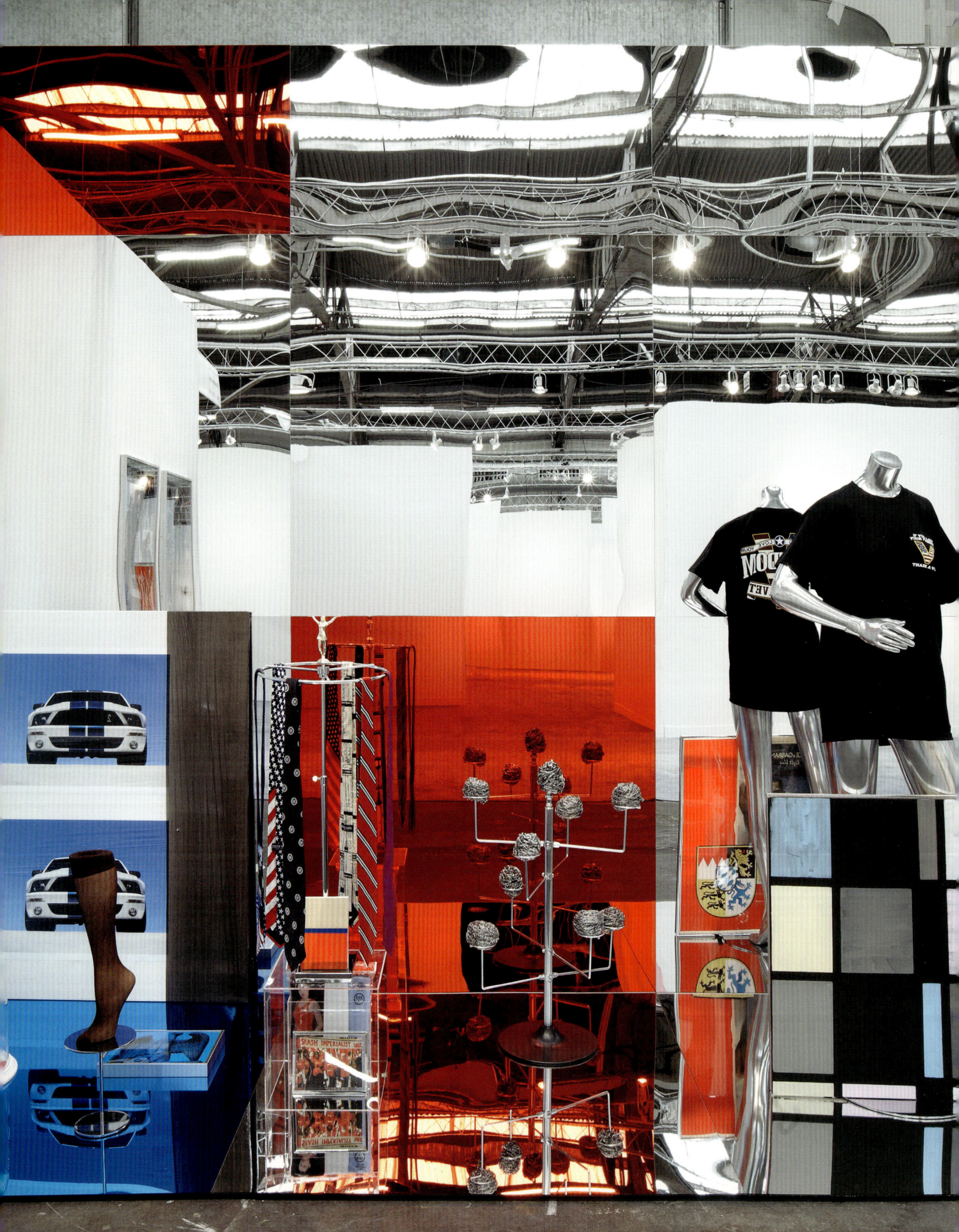

JOSEPHINE MECKSEPER
ARTIST

AMERICAN MALL

Fashion, like architecture, inheres in the darkness of the lived moment, belongs to the dream consciousness of the collective. The latter awakes, for example, in advertising.
—Walter Benjamin, *The Arcades Project*

The shopping mall has become the ultimate American landscape. It is modernity's epicenter of artificial leisure and activity, church and museum at once. Everything is on display: commodities, entertainment, military recruiting, and exploitation of the workforce. *American Mall* (2010, opposite page and pp. 84–85) chronicles the story of our late capitalist society. The collective performative aspect of consumption is frozen and reflected onto its mirrored platform.

The portrait of the mall is a speculation on our postindustrial consumer society and how it can be viewed as an archaeology of the present. There is no affirmative reassurance in the seemingly benign display forms and the objects that are presented on the reflective surface. The role of appropriated and recycled imagery and objects borrowed from popular culture and history is here to describe how the objects themselves become mere signifiers of mass consumption. The display installations and steel vitrines draw a direct correlation to the way our consumer culture has historically shaped cultural production and how early modernism and the avant-garde developed into a form of political and aesthetic resistance to an emerging capitalism.

In part inspired by the actions of the Seattle World Trade Organization protests in 1999, the focus on industrial retail aesthetics such as shop windows, shelves, and platforms in my work attempts to capture not only the actual protests but also the moment right before a demonstrator picks up a stone and vandalizes a store window. A sense of instability haunts the mirrored surfaces and the objects reflected in them, as if the reason for their existence is the anticipation of their own destruction—"Art at war with its own commodity character," as Walter Benjamin proposed.

I am looking for industrial and sociological endpoints as a signifier of our present state and the role of the artist in our consumer and post-Fordian society. How does one reconcile the symbolic and the monetary value of cultural production? How does one make visible informal economic and political realities without perpetuating them? Is there really still subversiveness in the appropriation of pop culture? Who will own the future? This is the narrative and the dialectical relationship between distance and proximity to consumer products and advertising in my work.

The story of our culture and time can be told in many ways. *American Mall* is one story, a way to create a window into our time. It's a speculation on our society and an investigation of the overall human condition and how the present state of this condition will be read and interpreted by coming generations. At a time when the manifestation and aesthetics of production and consumption are in a state of complete transition, exposing a new history of the object that has become free agent and is now arranging and rearranging reality for us.

—

Josephine Meckseper, *American Mall* (detail), 2010, mixed media, 120 × 282 × 48 in., courtesy of Andrea Rosen Gallery, New York

"SOMETHING DIFFERENT NEEDS TO BE DONE... SO THAT ART CONTINUES TO BE A PLACE TO RETHINK THE POLITICAL, TO SHIFT PERSPECTIVES."

—JAMES VOORHIES

JAMES VOORHIES
CURATOR

ART IN THE AGE OF LIBIDINAL DESIRE, OR RETURN THE CRITICAL TO POLITICAL ART

Now Is Our Time is the title of a video made in 2011 by the Portland-based advertising agency Wieden+Kennedy as part of Levi's global campaign "Go Forth."[1] The video begins with a series of shots of a young woman. Arms reaching toward the sky, she wears a black-feathered cape and stands on a ledge overlooking Paris, a city revered for its revolutionary spirit. The figure is reminiscent of a modern-day Nike of Samothrace, long admired as a symbol for struggle and perseverance. A swift succession of shots follow: close-ups of legs clad in denim and feet stomping across cobblestones; crimson smoke waffling over a street; a young man dressed completely in dark denim confronting a barricade of riot police. Rapturous images of young, beautiful people dancing, swimming, and kissing—accompanied by a seductive musical score and an assured male voice reciting a poem by Charles Bukowski[2]—sweep the video into its final crescendo where viewers are solemnly reminded: "the gods wait to delight in you." *Now Is Our Time* is frenetic, titillating, and libidinal. It gives the impression of an unstoppable youth culture on the verge of achieving something important. That, at least, is what Levi's wants us to believe—to sense and to feel.

Visual marketing to mass consumers is what pop art originally responded to in the 1950s and 1960s. We know the artists: Andy Warhol, James Rosenquist, Roy Lichtenstein, Robert Rauschenberg, Martha Rosler. They co-opted the glitz, finesse, color, editorial savvy, and zeal of mass advertising to make the marketing strategies their own. And they did it as part of an underlying critique of consumer culture and its influence on a rapidly changing world. Their work had political efficacy because they utilized the very form under scrutiny to destabilize it. How does art today retain political traction when corporations like Levi's take up the mission "to create positive change in the world" on their own terms and with "consumer sentiment" in mind?[3] In this particular case, visual marketing co-opts the aesthetics of protest culture, using the appearance of what is widely believed to be political art for its own capital gain and consumer audience. And the contemporary viewer is now more sophisticated precisely because of our familiarity with visual culture like the Levi's commercial. Our ability to synthesize complex intersections of commodity, media, and political culture has become too advanced for artists to believe that simply juxtaposing representations of war, chaos, and consumerism has the political capacity to create social change.

What is to be done? That's hardly answerable here; yet something different needs to be done, something that reframes the common experience of the spectator so that art continues to be a place to rethink the political, to shift perspectives. The situation calls for artists and institutions to create and support art that reflects the uncertainty and challenges of our contemporary life, an art that responds differently, just as pop art once did. The situation calls for art and exhibitions to be something other than what they are, for a belief that they don't have to be done like *that*. Criticality is not achieved by making work that looks political. As French philosopher Jacques Rancière astutely reminds us: "The main enemy of artistic creativity as well as of political creativity is consensus—that is, inscription within given roles, possibilities, and competences."[4]

In other words, yes, now is our time to do it differently.

—

1. The video has been viewed on Levi's YouTube channel by more than 3,700,000 people as of April 2, 2014, uploaded to numerous other sites, and televised in North America, Europe, and Asia. Levi's stores had corresponding in-store and window displays with the words "Now" "Is" "Our" "Time" on separate black placards placed behind mannequins wearing Levi's apparel.
2. The poem is "The Laughing Heart" (1996).
3. "Levi's Legacy," Wieden+Kennedy, http://www.wk.com/campaign/legacy.
4. In "Art of the Possible: Fulvia Carnevale and John Kelsey in Conversation with Jacques Rancière," *Artforum*, March 2007.

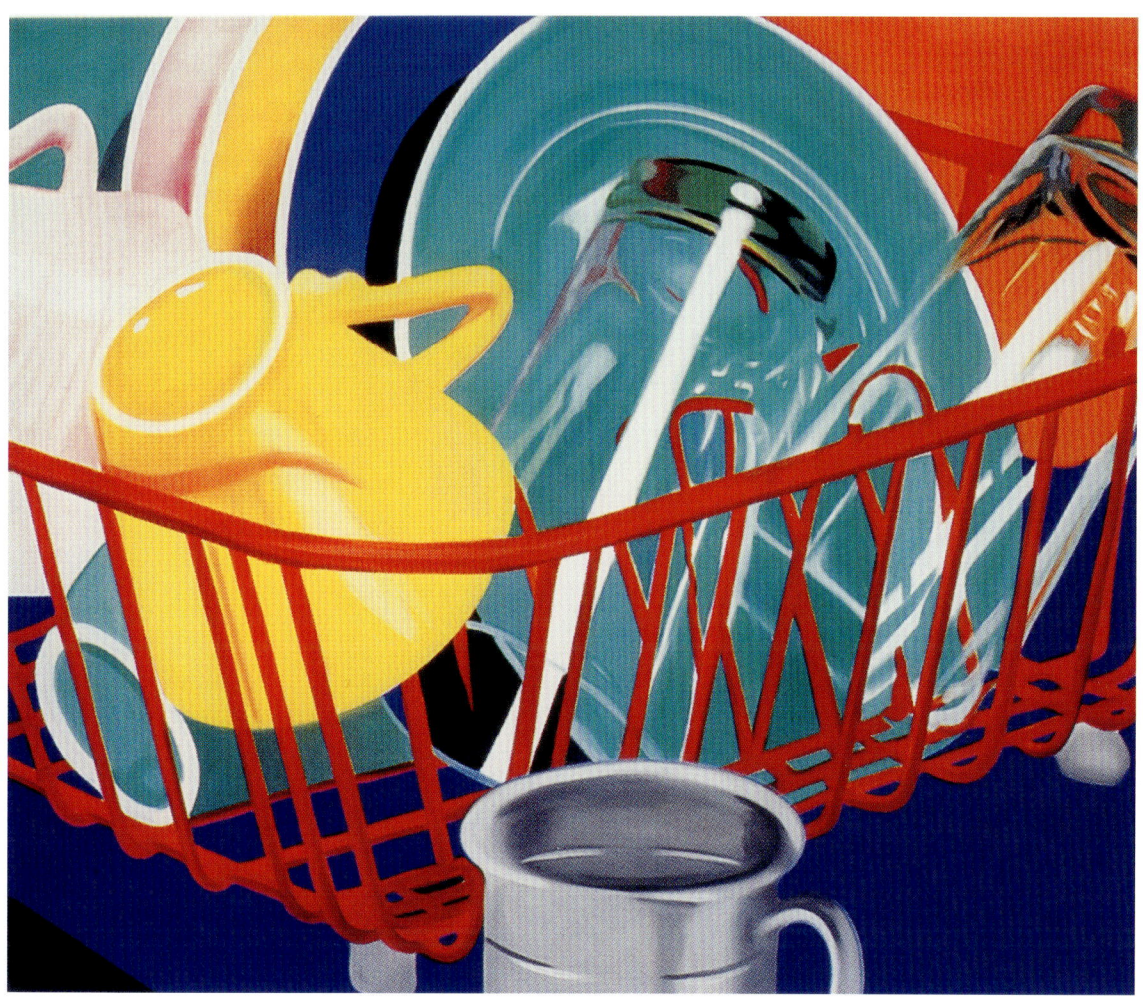

James Rosenquist, *Dishes*, 1964, oil on canvas, 50 × 60 in., Seattle Art Museum, Promised gift of the Virginia and Bagley Wright Collection, in honor of the 75th Anniversary of the Seattle Art Museum, © James Rosenquist / Licensed by VAGA, New York

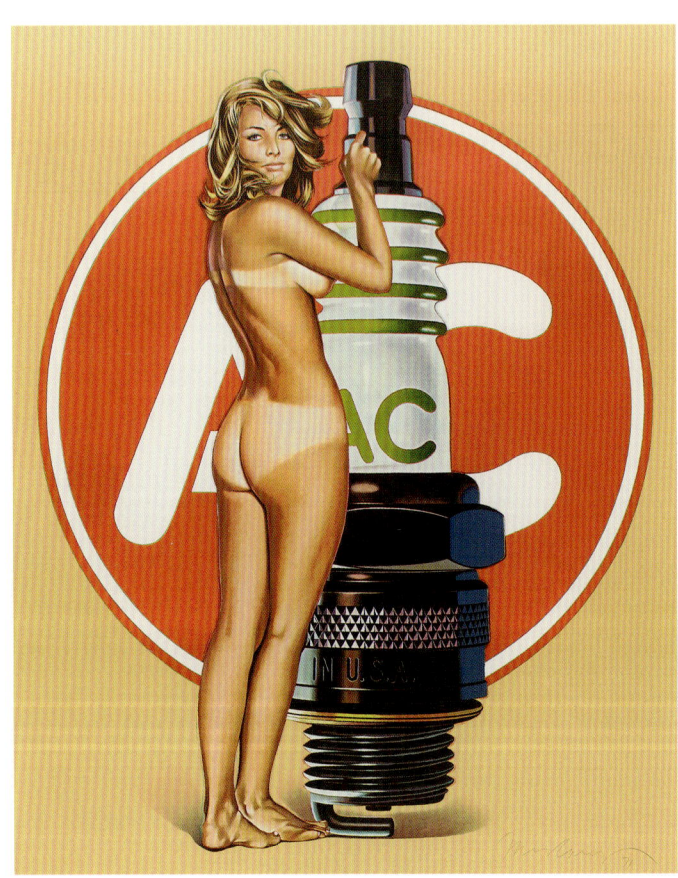

Mel Ramos, *AC Annie*, 1971, offset lithograph, 33¾ × 25⅛ in., Los Angeles County Museum of Art, Gift of Michael Asher and Pamela Sue Allen, AC1997.200.9, © Mel Ramos / Licensed by VAGA, New York

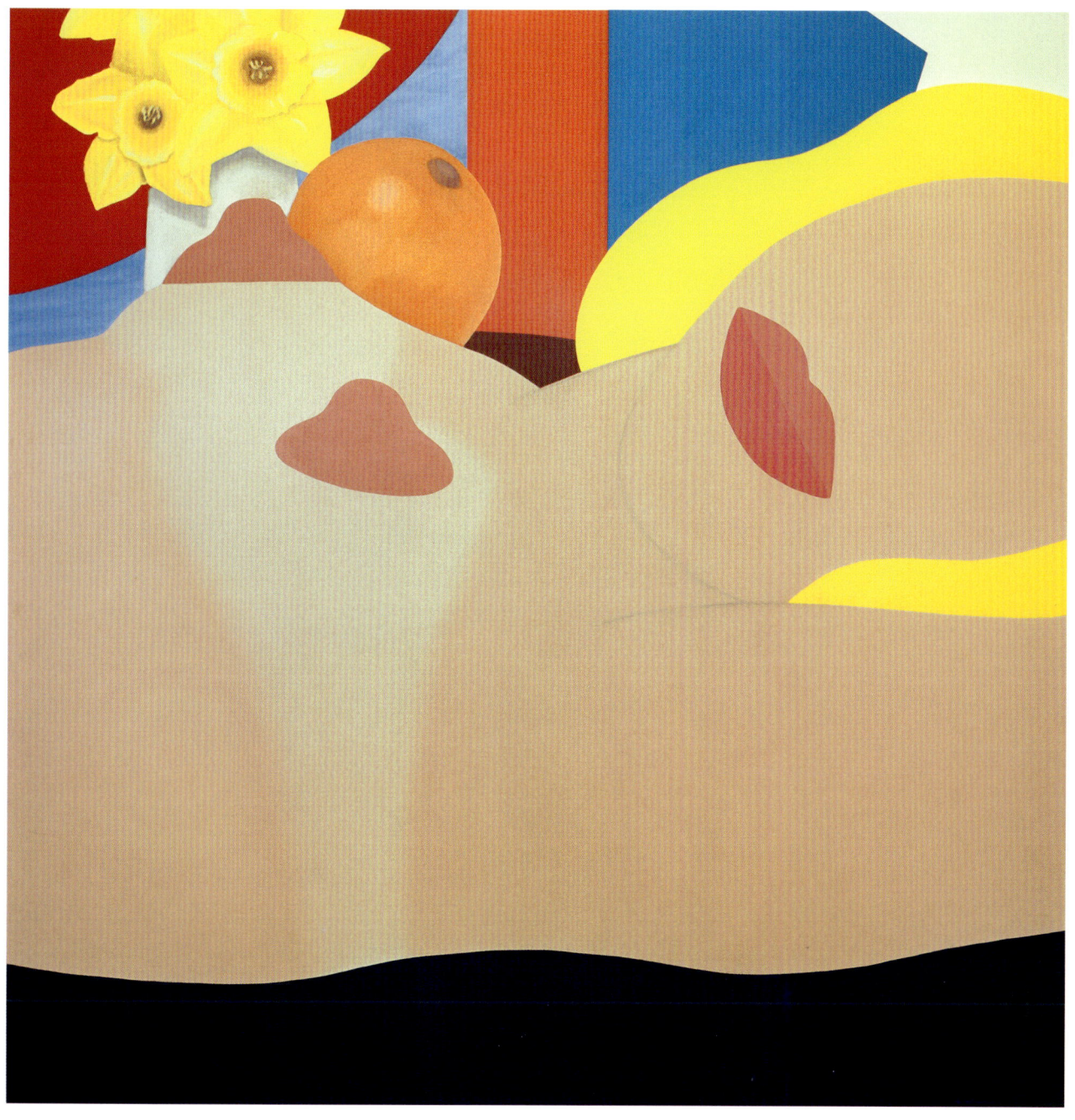

Tom Wesselmann, *Great American Nude No. 66*, 1965, oil and acrylic on canvas, 73 × 73½ in., Seattle Art Museum, Promised gift of the Virginia and Bagley Wright Collection, in honor of the 75th Anniversary of the Seattle Art Museum, © Estate of Tom Wesselmann / Licensed by VAGA, New York

Jeff Koons, *Pink Panther*, 1988, porcelain on Formica base, 41 × 20½ × 19 in., Museum of Contemporary Art, Chicago, Gerald S. Elliott Collection, 1995.57

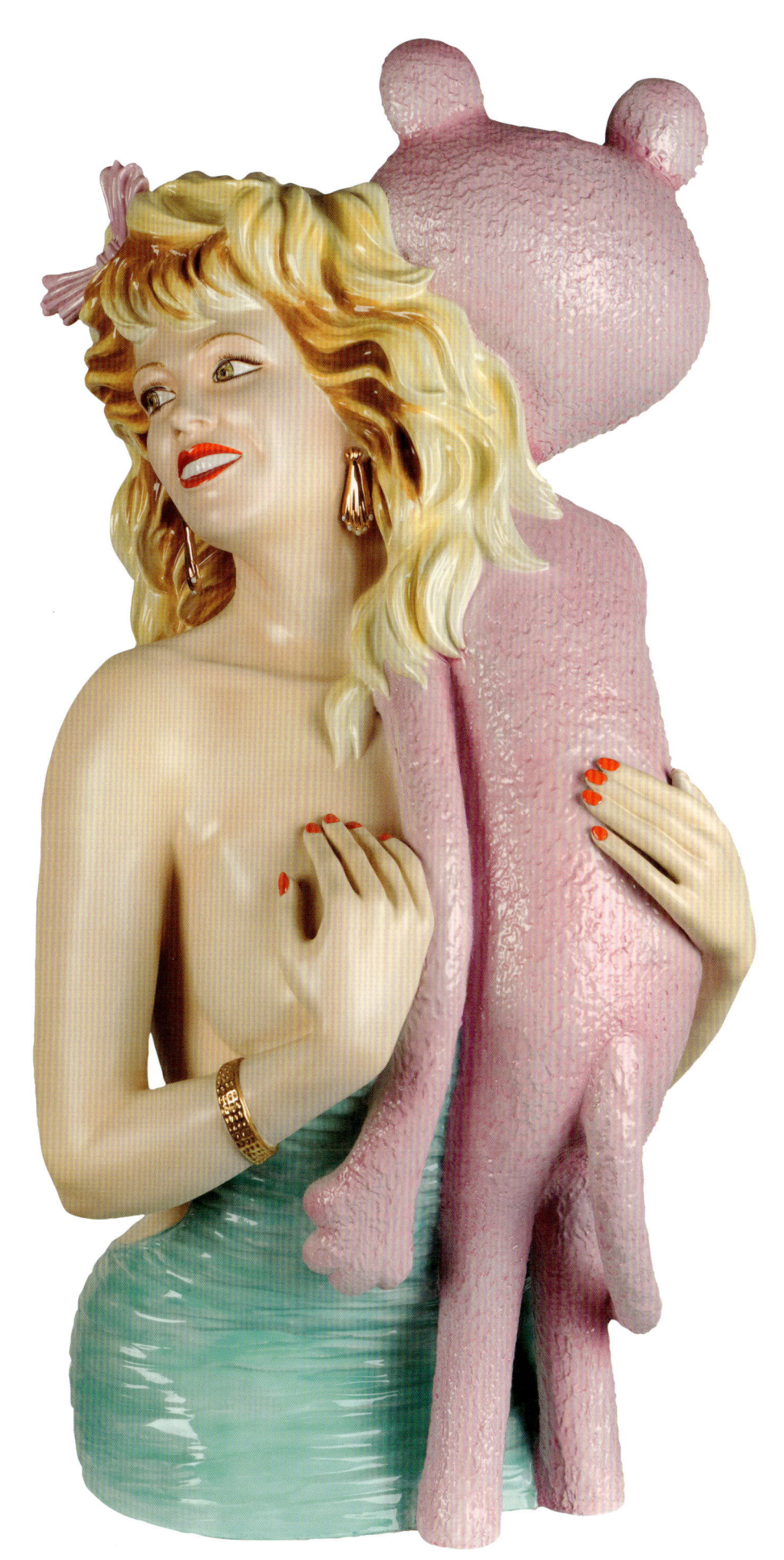

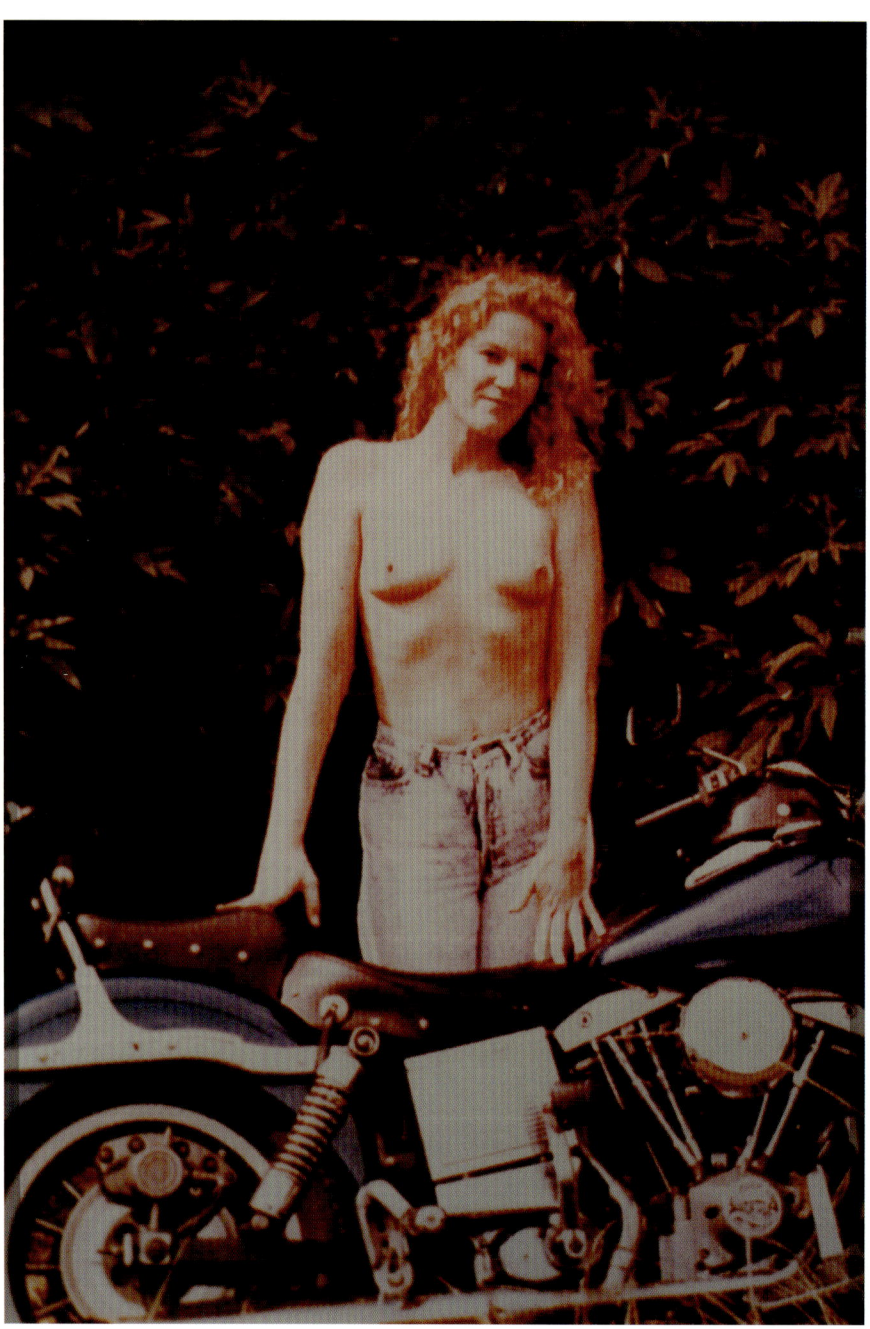

Richard Prince, *Untitled (Girlfriend)*, 1993, Ektacolor print, 64 × 44 in., private collection

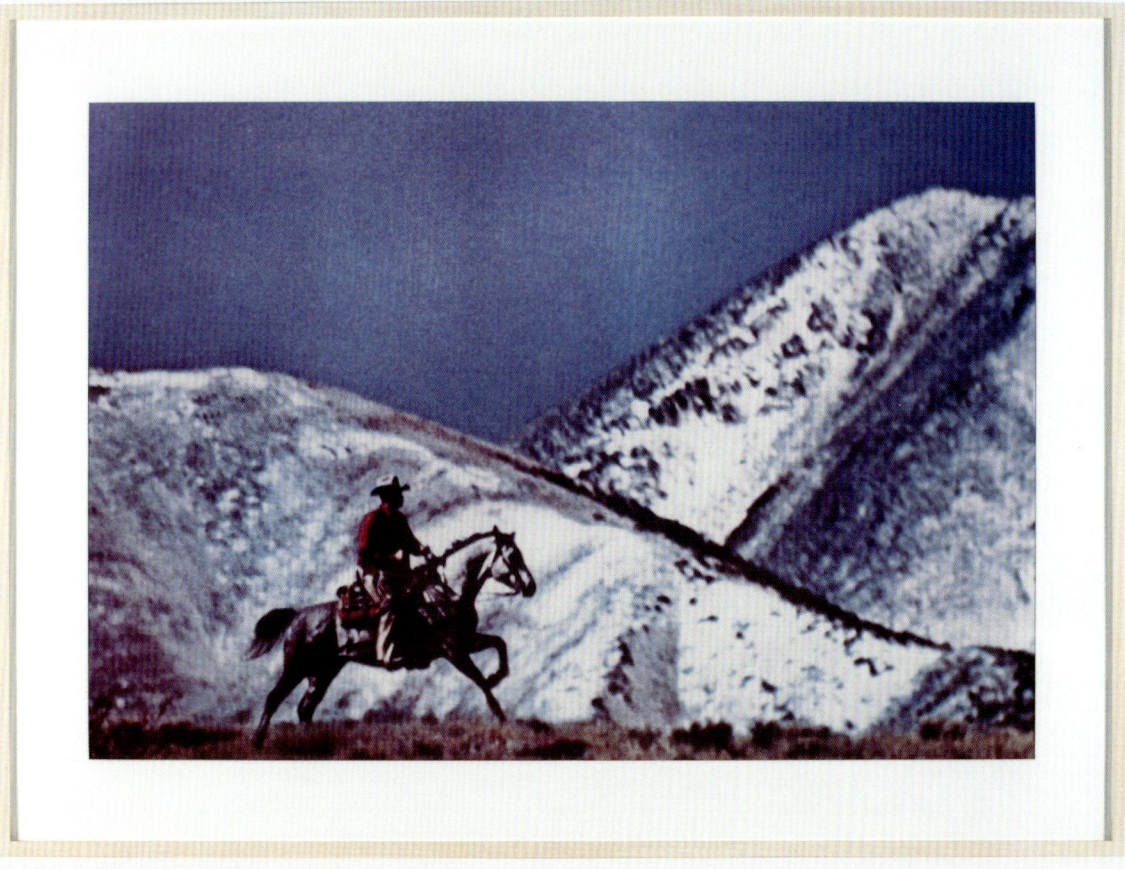

Richard Prince, *Untitled (Cowboys)*, 1980, Ektacolor print, 27 × 40 in., The Museum of Contemporary Art, Los Angeles, Purchased with funds provided by the National Endowment for the Arts, a Federal Agency, and Councilman Joel Wachs

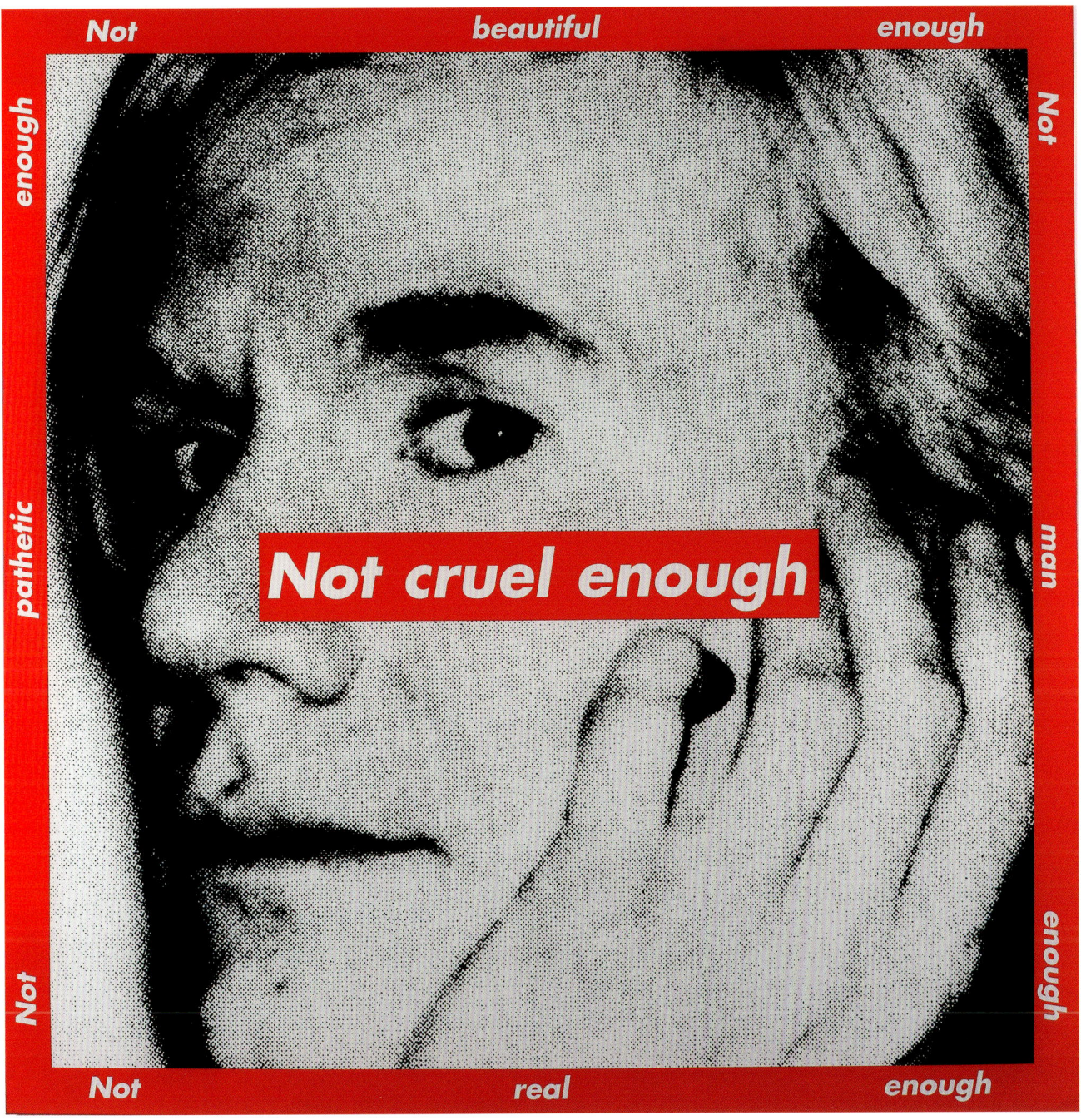

Barbara Kruger, *Untitled (Not cruel enough)*, 1997, photographic silkscreen on vinyl, 109 × 109 in., The Museum of Contemporary Art, Los Angeles, Gift of Vivian and Hans Buehler

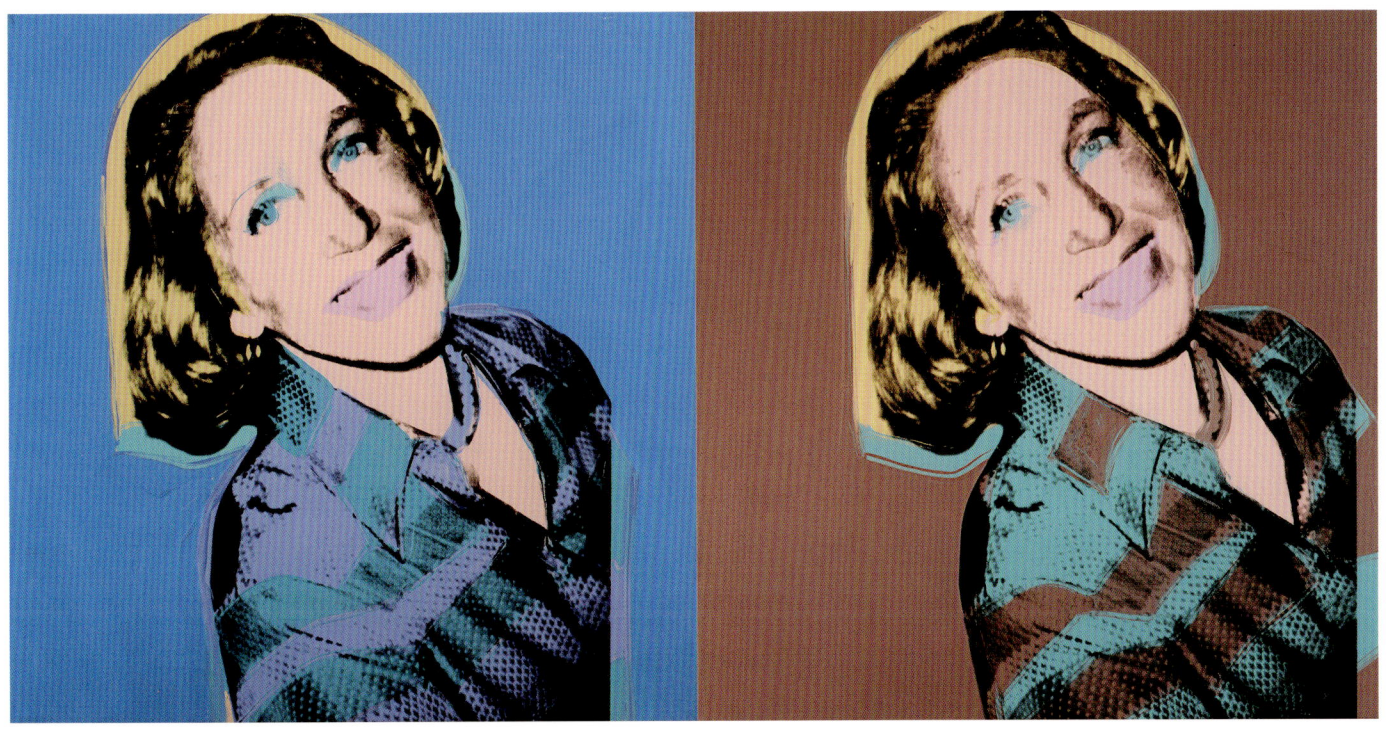

Andy Warhol, *Jane Lang Davis*, 1976, silkscreen ink, synthetic polymer paint on canvas, two panels, 40 × 40 in. each, Seattle Art Museum, Gift of Mr. and Mrs. Richard E. Lang, 76.47 (left panel), Collection of Jane Lang Davis (right panel)

Andy Warhol, *Two White Mona Lisas*, 1980, silkscreen polymer on canvas, 26½ × 40 in., Collection of Ann P. Wyckoff

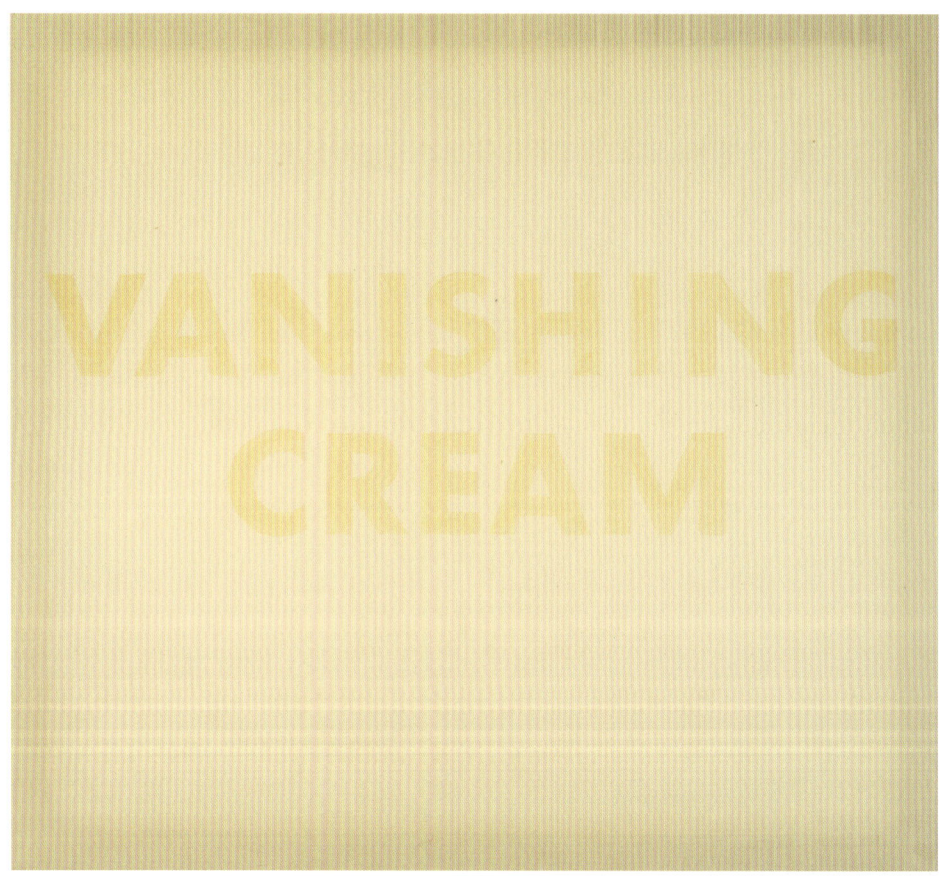

Ed Ruscha, *Vanishing Cream*, 1973, egg yolk on waterfall rayon, 35⅞ × 40 in., Seattle Art Museum, Promised gift of the Virginia and Bagley Wright Collection, in honor of the 75th Anniversary of the Seattle Art Museum

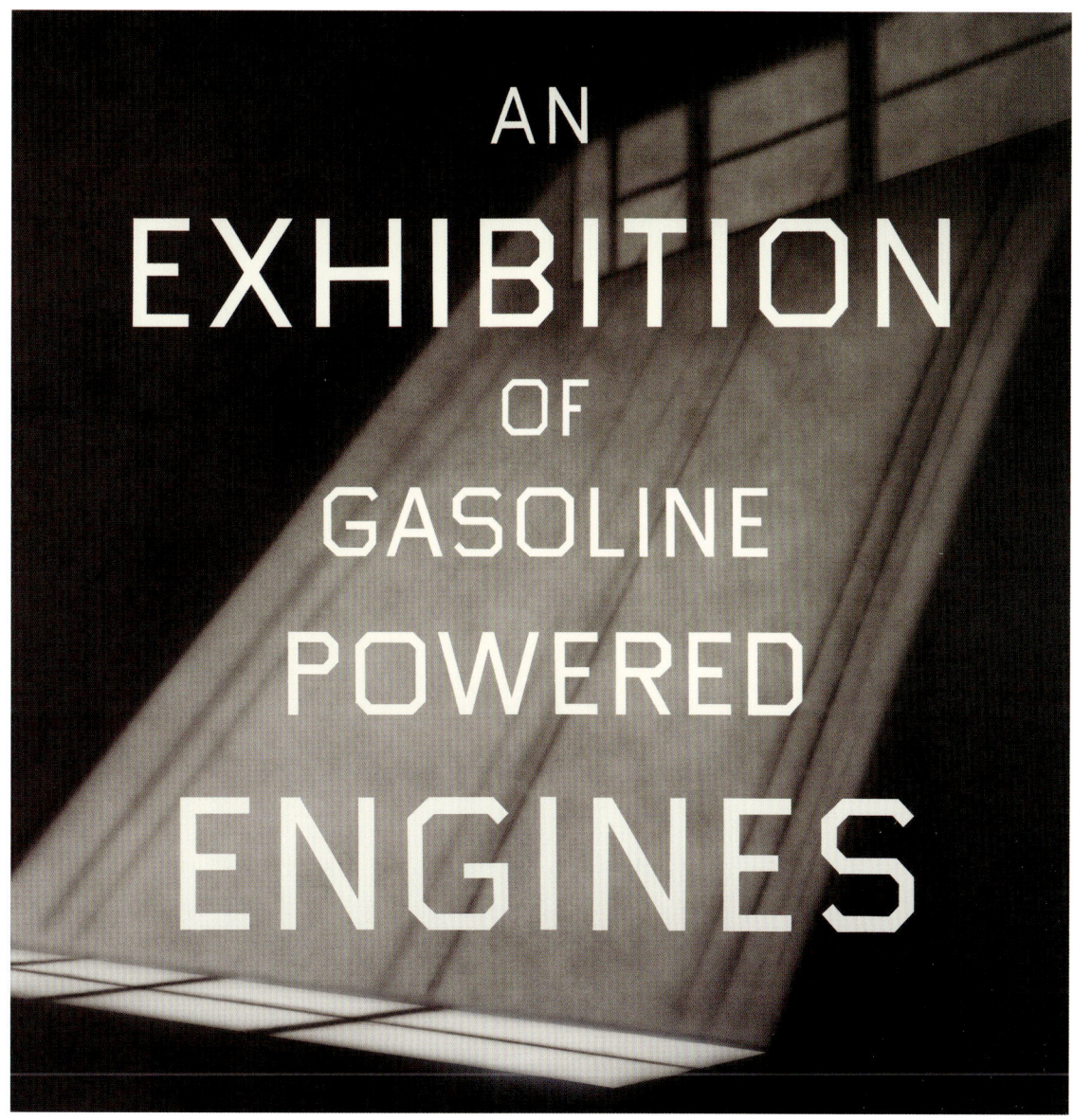

Ed Ruscha, *An Exhibition of Gasoline Powered Engines*, 1993, acrylic on linen, 84 × 84 in., Seattle Art Museum, Jeffrey and Susan Brotman, Mary Alice and Dick Cooley, Jane and David Davis, Robert Dootson, Lyn and Jerry Grinstein, Ann and John H. Hauberg, Mimi and Vinton Sommerville, Mary and Dean Thornton, Carol Wright, and the Margaret E. Fuller Purchase Fund, 98.52

Nam June Paik, *Attila the Hun*, 1993, mixed media, 96½ × 39¾ × 80¾ in., Collection of Jon Shirley

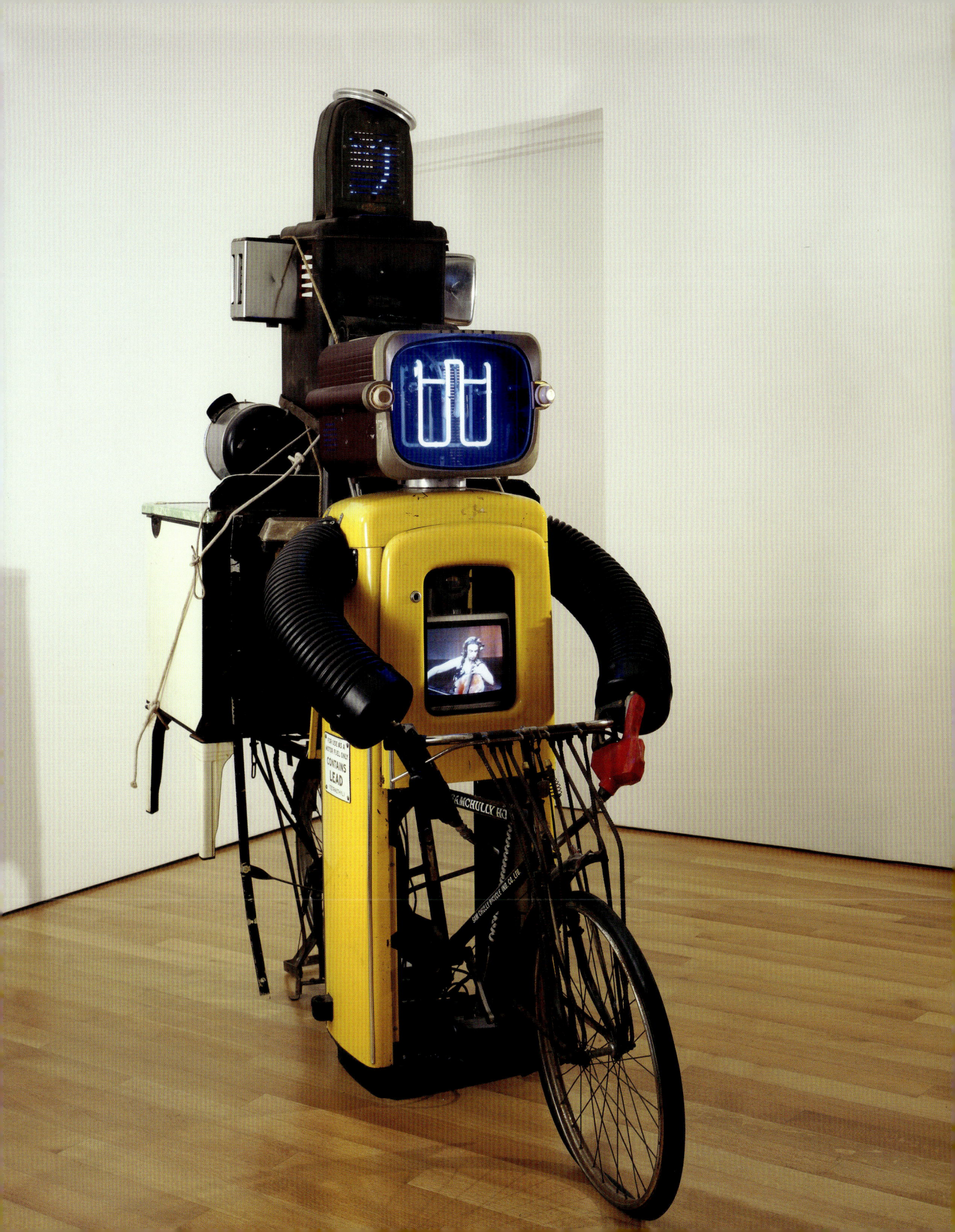

THE TERROR OF IMMORTALITY

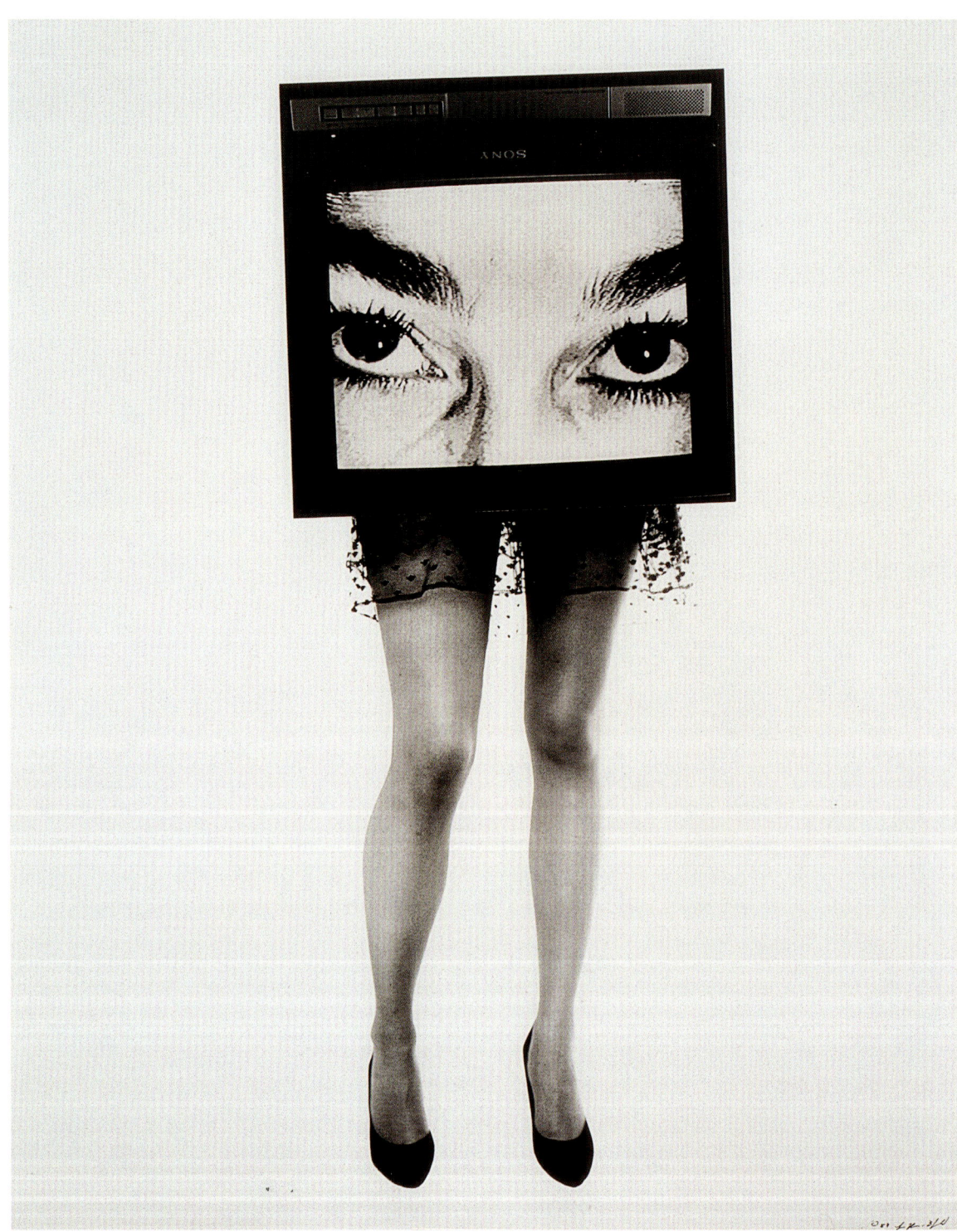

Lynn Hershman Leeson, *TV Legs* from *The Phantom Limb* series, 1987, gelatin silver photograph, 24 × 20 in., Seattle Art Museum, Gift of Rod Slemmons, 95.79

LYNN HERSHMAN LEESON

ARTIST AND FILMMAKER

THE TERROR OF IMMORTALITY

In *The Phantom Limb* series (opposite page), anthropomorphic photographs merge human bodies with reproductive machinery such as cameras, monitors, and cathode-ray tubes. This work references the invasive nature of mass media and the ingestion of images that ultimately alters our mental projection of identity. Robotic appendages address an evolving, technologically assisted human existence. The implicit strategy of these robotic female cyborgs is that they are posed and poised to outwit their captors. They are complicit in the action and understand fully what is being done to them, and therefore they seek to avenge themselves by reversing, revising, and transforming the very dynamic of absorption and consumption, seduction and defiance.

Capture systems are endemic to our society, and images are among the things they capture. About 1.2 billion photographs are made per day. Many of these images are authorless, created through robot-driven surveillance systems. Surveillance footage and capture systems are the hired guns, the saviors and savers of cultural history. Excess becomes the armature of junk culture, built by invisible coders and composted into an ever-growing aesthetics of consumption.

Does surveillance invite security or create fear? Are capture systems built for safety or aggression? Who is watching whom? What will be preserved? Who has the power to make these decisions? And what happens when capture systems such as jpgs, tiffs, and video become obsolete? Images in fact have become vulnerable because of their availability and mutability.

Capture systems aren't limited to images. Cyborgian mythology was reborn with a vengeance when, recently, live cells were placed in 3D bio printers. This methodology extends the photographic process into developing and printing synthetic organs and skin. These interwoven strands of time and lineage create a fresh cyborgian identity, a hyper-simulation that simultaneously extends living systems while posing a lethal threat to "nature." Skin and organs emerge pulsating and fully formed through accessible photographic printing equipment. The process of photo printing is such a powerful medium that it not only analyzes the hybridity of cultural aesthetic but extends the dialogue to life itself.

Reproductive technological parts in my photography of the 1980s (including *The Phantom Limb* series) sprouted from the image of the female, creating a cyborgian reformation as parts of the real body disappear. My current work addresses the physical creation and/or erasure of body parts through absorption of mutated or reconfigured DNA or genetic protein. The organic process is dynamically reshaping the identity of the newly cultured organisms, as well as the culture of absorbed surveillance.

APPROPRIATION IN A CONSTRUCTED WORLD

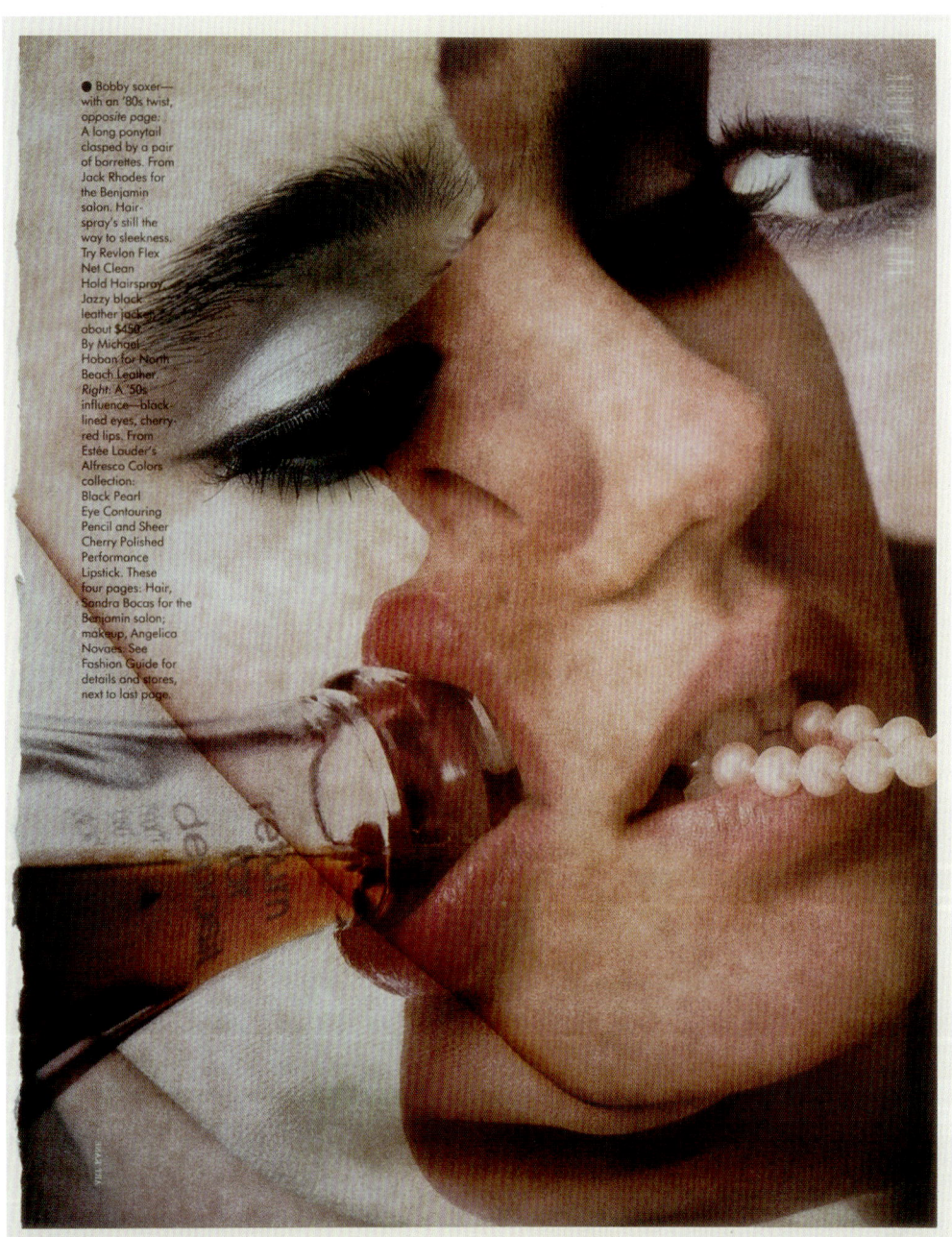

Robert Heinecken, *Recto/Verso #7*, 1988, cibachrome photogram, 14 × 11 in., Seattle Art Museum, Richard E. Lang Modern Acquisition Fund and the Margaret E. Fuller Purchase Fund, 90.31.1.7

ANNE ELLEGOOD
CURATOR

APPROPRIATION IN A CONSTRUCTED WORLD

The group of American artists that emerged onto the contemporary art scene in the late 1970s and early 1980s—later dubbed the "pictures generation"[1]—are, in my opinion, a distinct departure from pop art. Like the pop artists of the 1960s, the pictures generation was noteworthy, in part, because of the artists' embrace of the strategy of appropriation, the borrowing (or stealing, as Dara Birnbaum has asserted) and recontextualizing of existing images and forms from available cultural sources including newspapers, magazines, widely available commodities, and indeed, art history. Yet despite this shared impulse, their intentions were, in fact, quite different. More than an argument for bringing the "low" forms of culture—from cartoons strips to celebrity headshots—into the lauded domain of high art's most cherished medium, painting, the pictures generation felt the unrelentingly forceful hegemony of these cultural institutions and wanted to take back control. This was the first generation in American history for whom television viewing became normative, for the TV was now a ubiquitous presence in the American middle-class home. Artists such as Dara Birnbaum and Gretchen Bender were fully aware, and extremely critical, of the influence of this predominant form of media. Others, among them Barbara Kruger and Robert Heinecken, took both content and visual language from newspapers and magazines to reveal their powerful ability to influence opinion, desire, and behavior. For these artists, it was not enough to recognize that mass media, or popular culture, were worthy subjects for the visual arts. Rather, they felt that art must be a domain where these forms are deconstructed and evaluated, revealing the mainstream ideologies in which they traffic.

Pop artists borrowed their imagery and then reasserted their authorship by developing signature styles rooted in the use of specific techniques.[2] The pictures generation's commitment to appropriation, in contrast, grew out of their skepticism about the belief in individuality, autonomous subjectivity, and genius that had been attached to notions of authorship for centuries. Their aim was to undermine this convention and call into question the very idea of originality, pointing, instead, to the ways in which every gesture is inscribed with those that came before. They argued that, as Crimp articulated, "underneath each picture there is always another picture."[3] Although it is sometimes difficult to locate the criticality within the lustful desire for consumerism inscribed in the works of Jeff Koons and Richard Prince, certainly other artists of this generation who took up the Duchampian embrace of the readymade by introducing found objects into their works, as well as those who produced rather than purchased recognizable forms, were less interested in a critique of capitalism per se than in specific processes that reside at the heart of how art operates within our culture. Haim Steinbach's earliest shelf pieces, for example, presented the personal curios of his friends on quirky customized shelves, and his interest in what, and more importantly *why*, people collect and keep objects remains paramount to his practice. By casting familiar forms—the urn, the vase, the framed painting—and presenting them in oftentimes dense groupings, Allan McCollum draws from industrial production methods to create objects that are simultaneously singular and multiples. The pictures generation artists recognized that art is ideological, and therefore, political. Pop artists *reflected* the popular culture around them; artists of this later generation set out to *intervene* into the entrenched power dynamics they witnessed around them. As Sherrie Levine recalled, "we wanted to make a difference, to show some resistance to the status quo."[4] Much more than a commodity or a strictly formal investigation, art is understood as a space of criticality with the potential to produce actual change.

---

1. The term "pictures generation" assigned to these artists was taken from the title (*Pictures*) of a 1977 exhibition curated by art historian and critic Douglas Crimp at Artists Space in New York City. Crimp's exhibition sought to articulate a shared impulse on the part of a young generation of artists who were freely borrowing images (or "pictures") from cultural sources—films, newspapers, television, advertising, and books—in works that were greatly influenced by photography and its capacity for infinite duplication and wide circulation. In their work, these artists were arguing that art is inscribed with layers of historical and contemporary references and is inevitably derived from a shared, collective field of images, forms, and knowledge. See Douglas Crimp, "Pictures," *October*, Spring 1979, 75–88; reprinted in *Art after Modernism: Rethinking Representation*, ed. Brian Wallis (New York: New Museum of Contemporary Art, 1984), 175–87.
2. Warhol's turn to silkscreening; Lichtenstein's adoption of the Ben-Day dot used in printing; Oldenburg's soft sculptures.
3. Crimp, "Pictures," in Wallis, *Art after Modernism*, 186.
4. "Sherrie Levine Talks to Howard Singerman," *Artforum*, April 2003.

CAPITALIST REALISM

"YOUNG ARTISTS TODAY… GO BEYOND SIMPLE APPROPRIATION… REVEALING HOW THE DIGITAL IS INSCRIBED INTO OUR BODIES AND OUR THINKING."

—ELODIE EVERS

ELODIE EVERS
CURATOR

CAPITALIST REALISM

The events that took place under the label "Capitalist Realism" in Germany during the early 1960s are still resonant, current, and topical today. Back then, a group of art students gathered at the Düsseldorf art academy who would soon end the victory lap of abstract painting. Unlike their contemporaries who favored gestural abstraction, these artists incorporated the trivia of everyday life and involved the audience. The protagonists—Gerhard Richter, Sigmar Polke, and Konrad Lueg—became pioneers of a German pop art that was heavily influenced by fluxus. *The First Exhibition of German Pop-Art* was the self-assured title of their 1963 pop-up exhibition at Kaiserstrasse 31A in Düsseldorf, a former butcher shop. A few months later, Richter and Lueg mounted their equally programmatic and legendary happening *Life with Pop: A Demonstration for Capitalist Realism* in a Düsseldorf furniture store. The artists hung their paintings like decoration in the furniture display area and placed themselves on pedestals while they watched the German evening news. The intervention is especially remarkable because it intertwined several concerns of pop art and fluxus: the combination of art and everyday life, the inclusion of the visitor, the critique of a bourgeois consumer culture, and the ironic use of their own artworks and their status as artists.

Like Andy Warhol, the German artists invested in the development of an artistic image in order to better market themselves. The departure for this undertaking was the German postwar era, which was defined by a burgeoning economic miracle but also by the horrors of the war years—which remained largely unarticulated and repressed. Like American pop artists, the German artists found their subjects in magazines and newspapers. They were concerned with dealing with the banal, everyday world, more precisely with its representation in photographs and media images. The approach of the artists to capitalism was likewise ambivalent: On the one hand they appreciated its emancipatory potential and made deliberate use of its marketing strategies in order to further their artistic careers. Simultaneously, however, they also staged the inherent vulgarity of capitalism in their paintings.

Although pop art's painted versions of reproductions foreshadowed the end of artistic originality (as traditionally defined) and introduced a new artistic model, many of the pop artists still used the classic medium of painting. Twenty years later, and differences notwithstanding, the American "pictures generation" again borrowed existing image material for their art. These artists, who were the heirs of pop, belonged to a generation that was born into a media-determined reality. For them, the media replaced reality. Strongly influenced by postmodern theories, they left behind criteria such as authorship and originality. Instead, their task was to probe the power of images and to reveal images' mechanisms of seduction using appropriated advertising imagery. The pictures generation artists focused on the crucial realization that the production and reception of pictures was ideologically coded, an insight that has helped shape today's artistic discourse on "digital natives" and "post-Internet artists."

The digital media, which are inseparable from the current manifestations of capitalism, determine contemporary artistic production unlike anything else. The Internet has allowed for a proletarianization of means of production, but it has also enforced the control of its use by a few monopolists and states but first and foremost private enterprises. Young artists today appropriate images they find online and thus continue certain readymade and pop traditions. But they go beyond simple appropriation, by introducing diverse translation processes that animate or anthropomorphize the found image, revealing how the digital is inscribed into our bodies and our thinking. Now, at a time when "Capitalist Realism" can be understood as a basic tenor or prevailing mood, we can recognize a turn toward the performative: contemporary artworks do not content themselves in quoting from the image world of capitalism; they allow for its more complex experience in order to reconquer and control the networks in which we are moving.

—

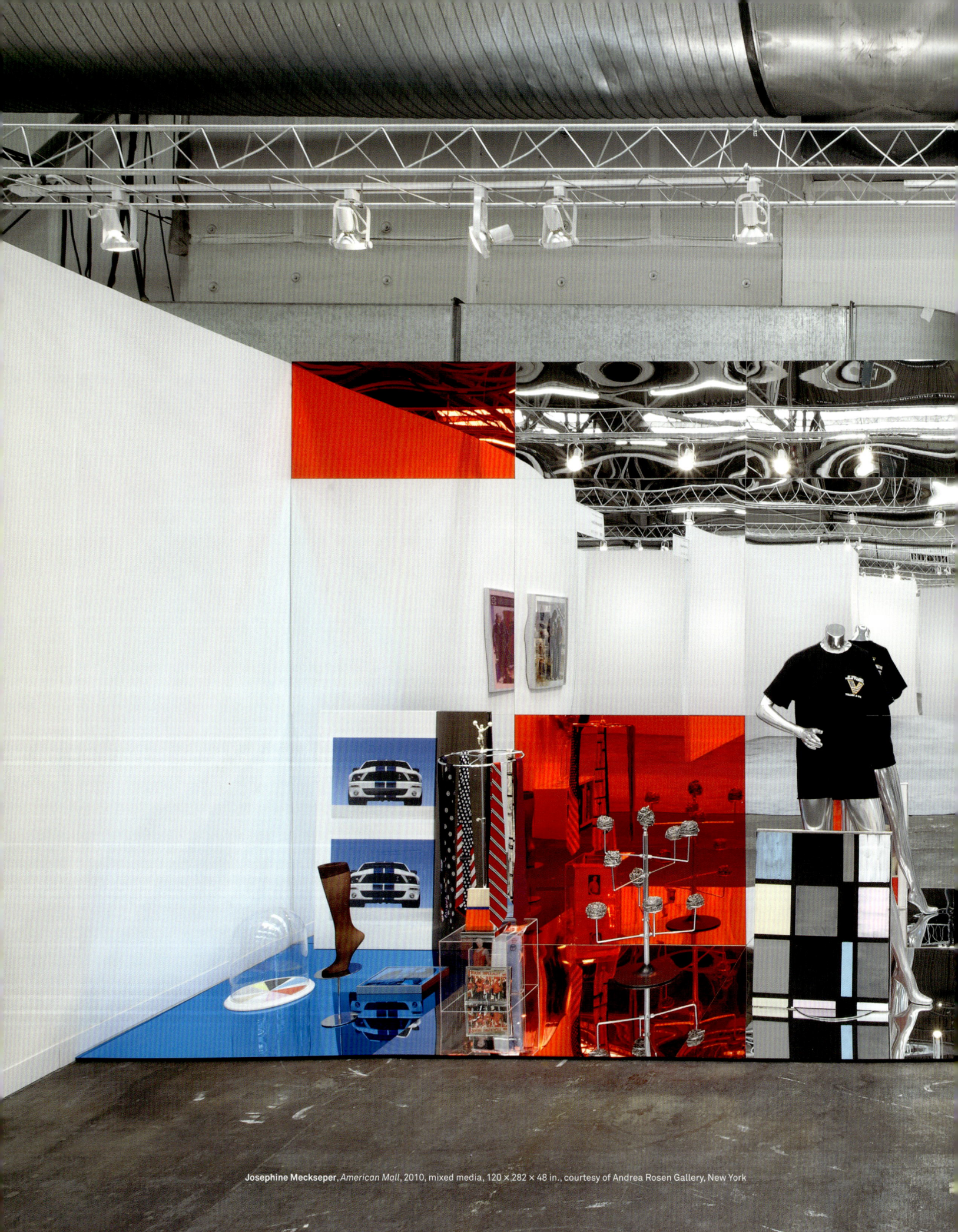

Josephine Meckseper, *American Mall*, 2010, mixed media, 120 × 282 × 48 in., courtesy of Andrea Rosen Gallery, New York

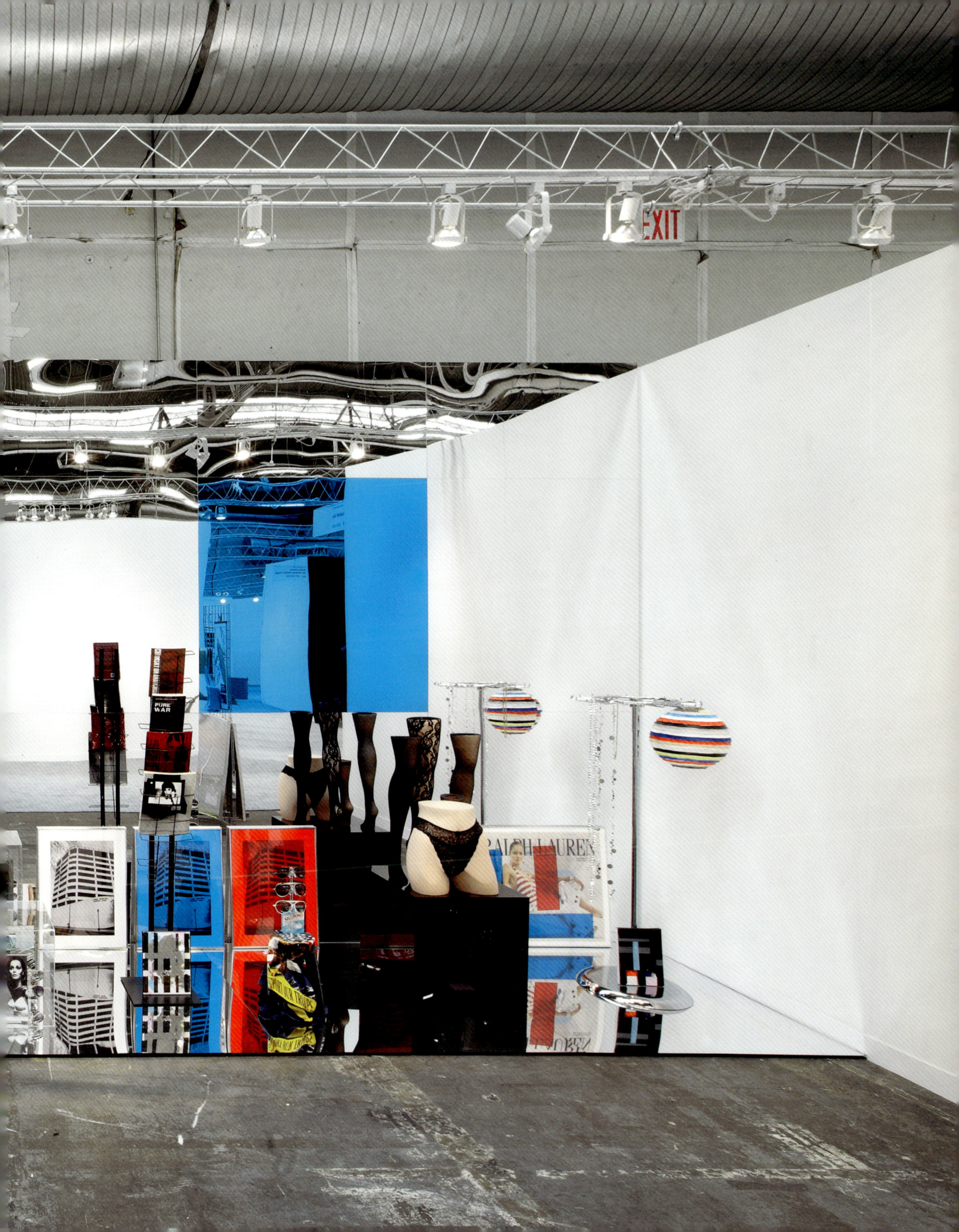

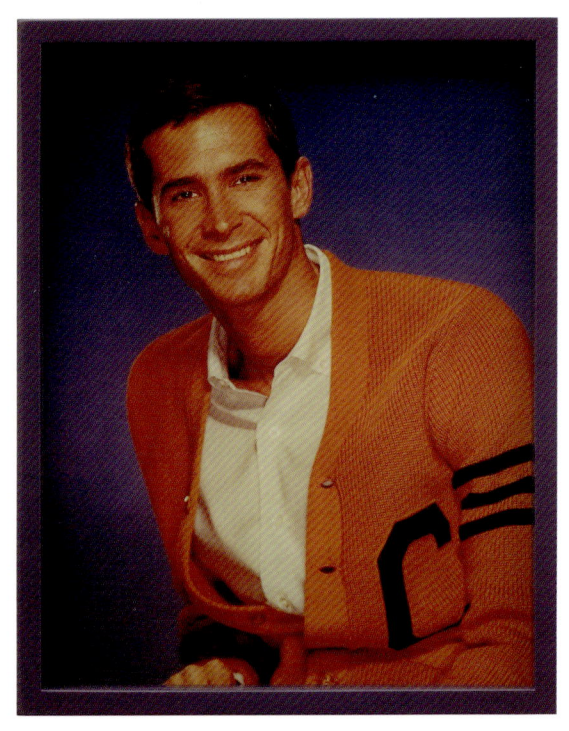
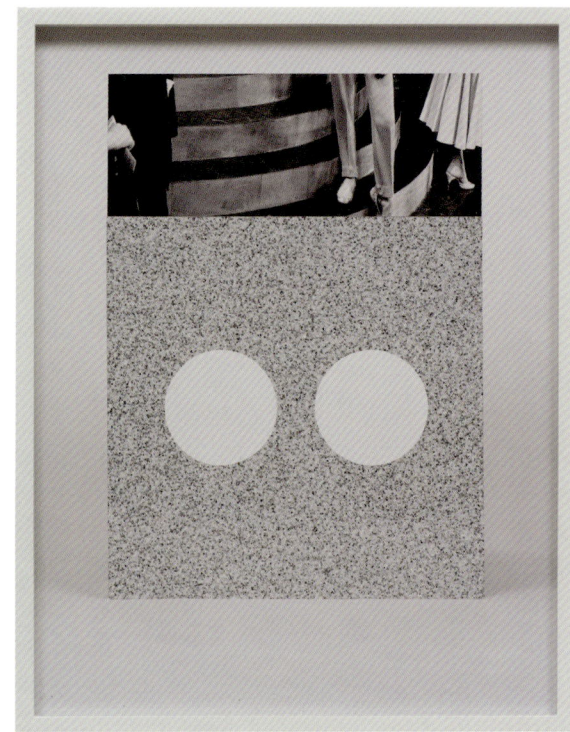
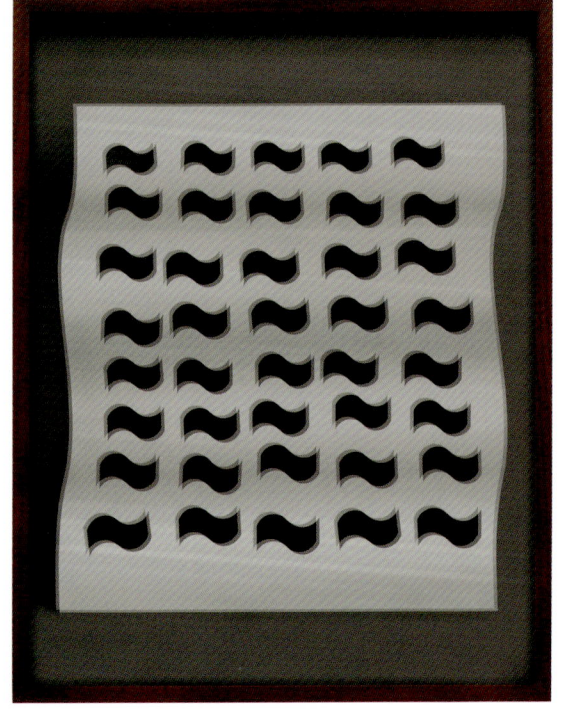
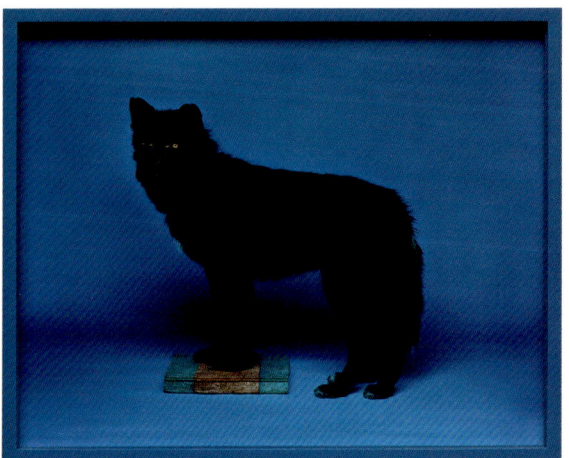

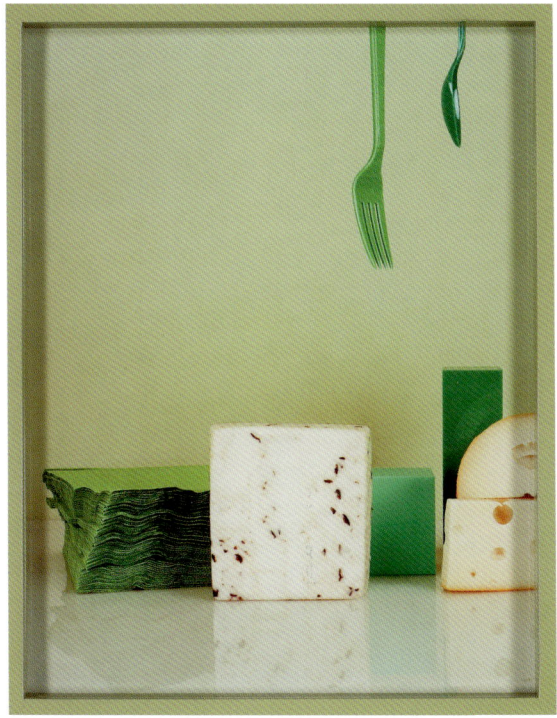
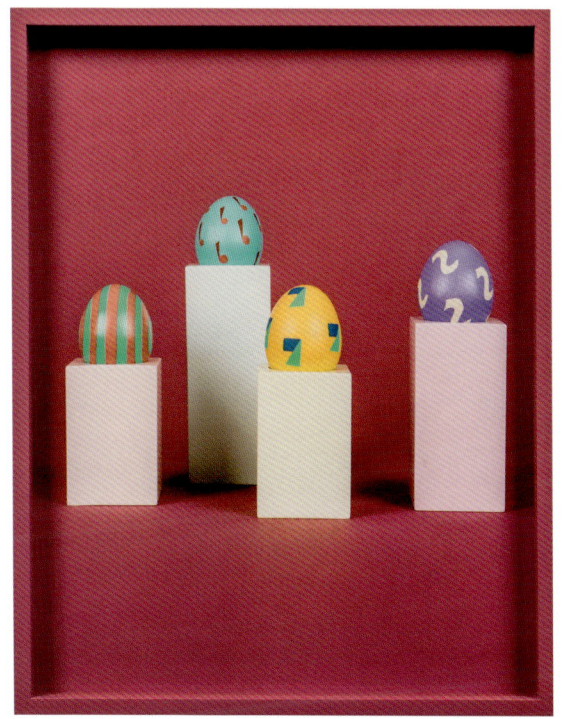
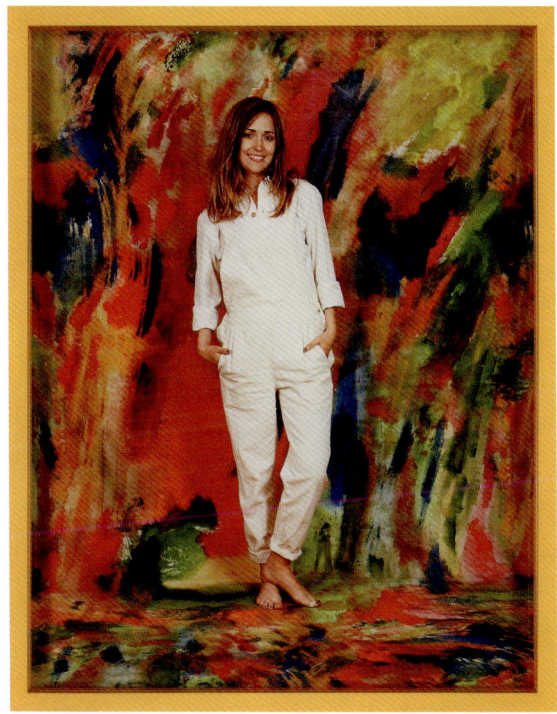

Elad Lassry

Portrait, Purple, 2008, C-print, painted frame, 10½ × 8½ × 1½ in., Collection of Kai Loebach

Wave 90046, 2013, silver gelatin print, walnut frame, 14 × 11½ × 1½ in., courtesy of the artist and David Kordansky Gallery, Los Angeles

Laminated Structure (For Stage), 2013, silver gelatin print on C-print, painted frame, 14 × 11½ × 1½ in., courtesy of the artist and David Kordansky Gallery, Los Angeles

Wolf (Blue), 2008, C-print, painted frame, 11½ × 14 × 1½ in., courtesy of David Kordansky and Mindy Shapiro, Los Angeles

Truffle Goat Cheese, Emmentaler, Fork and Spoon, 2010, C-print, painted frame, 14 × 11½ × 1½ in., courtesy of David Kordansky and Mindy Shapiro, Los Angeles

Woman (Painting), 2010, C-print, painted frame, 14 × 11½ × 1½ in., courtesy of David Kordansky and Mindy Shapiro, Los Angeles

Four Eggs, 2013, C-print, painted frame, 14 × 11½ × 1½ in., courtesy of David Kordansky and Mindy Shapiro, Los Angeles

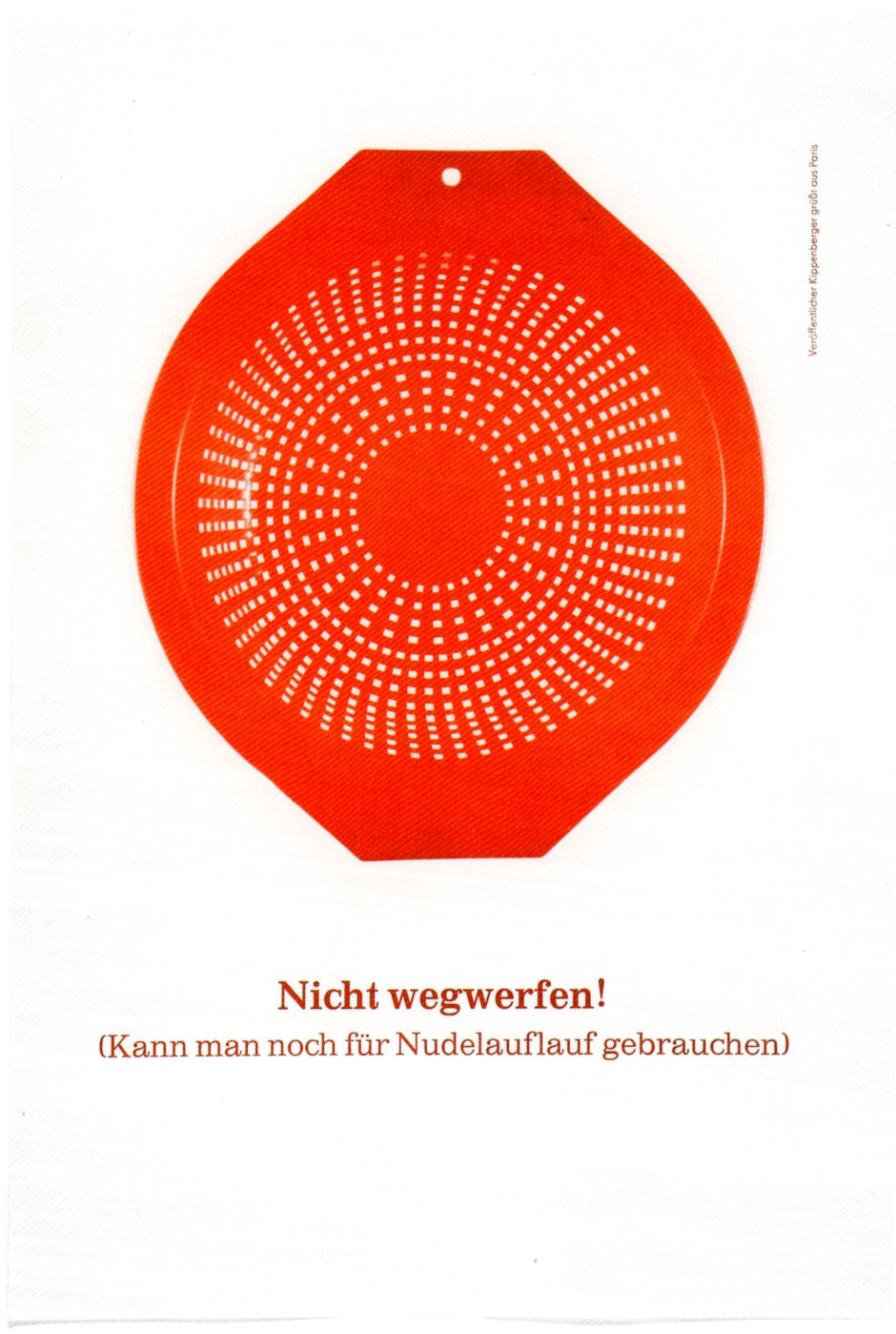

Martin Kippenberger, *Nicht wegwerfen! (Kann man noch für Nudelauflauf gebrauchen) (Don't Toss! [Can Still Be Used for Noodle Casserole])*, Berlin 1980, offset, 17 × 12 in., Collection of Jeffrey and Susan Brotman

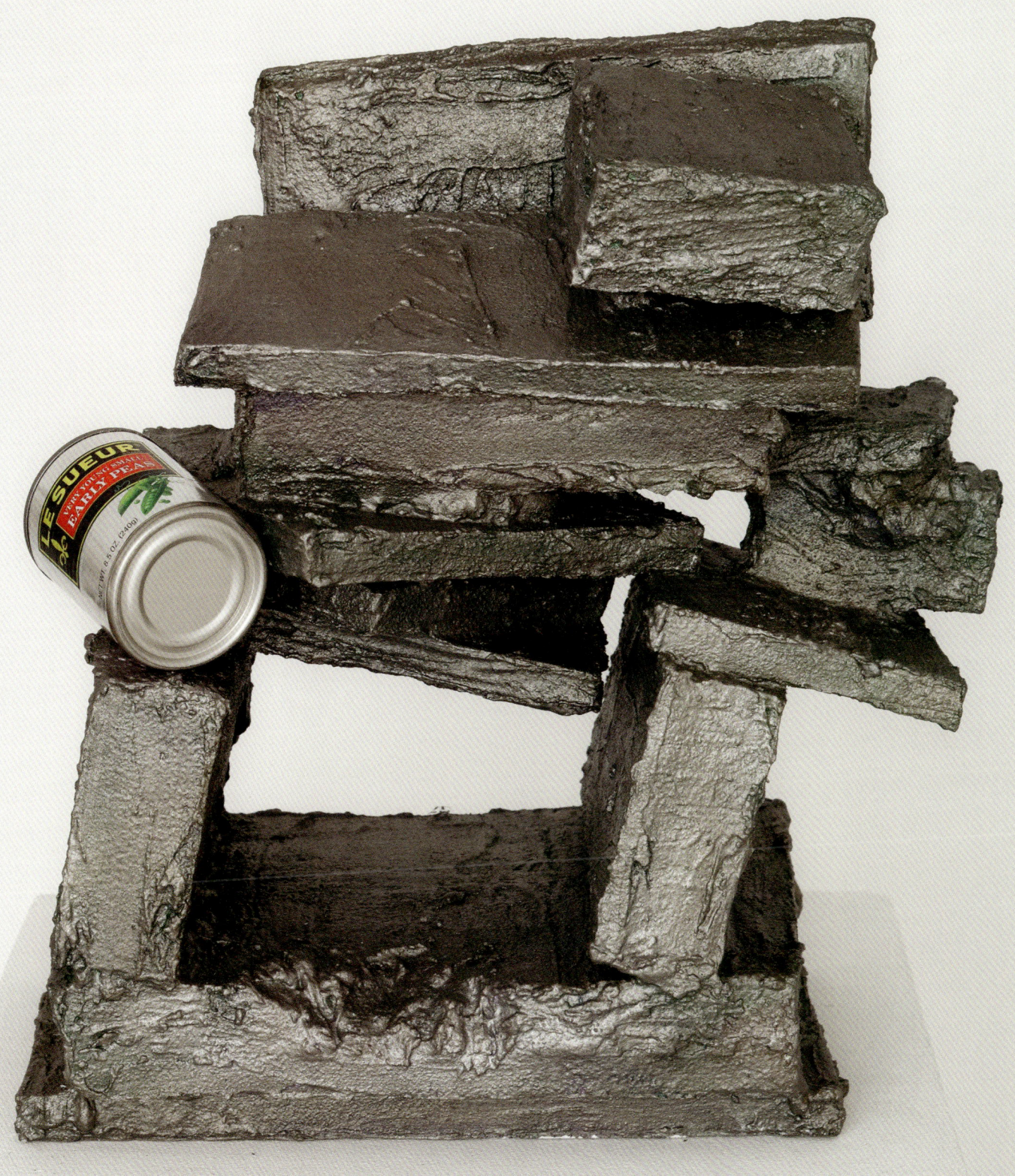

Rachel Harrison, *Very Young Small*, 2005, cast resin, acrylic, and peas, 16¾ × 16¼ × 9¼ in., courtesy of the artist and Greene Naftali, New York

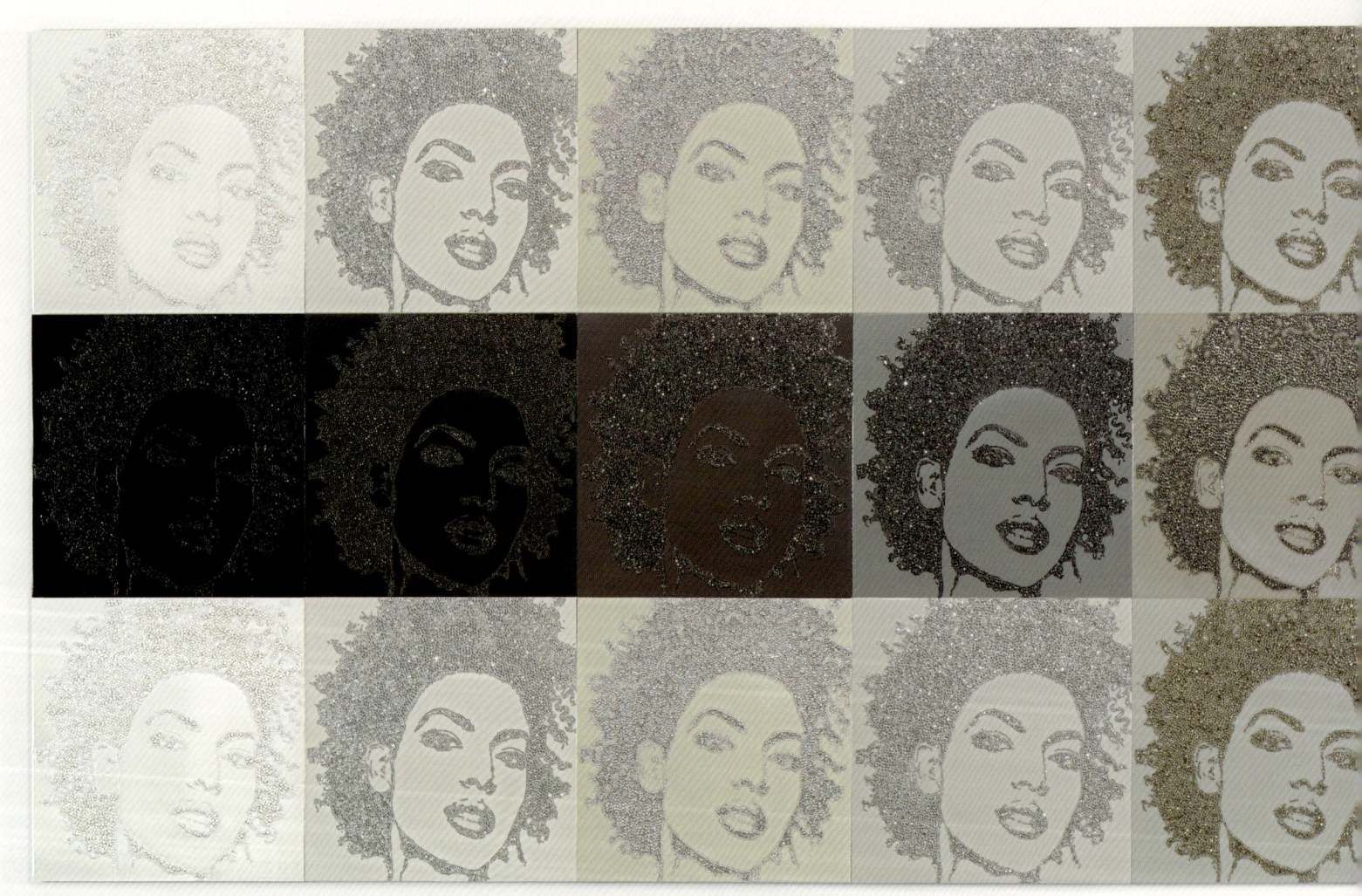

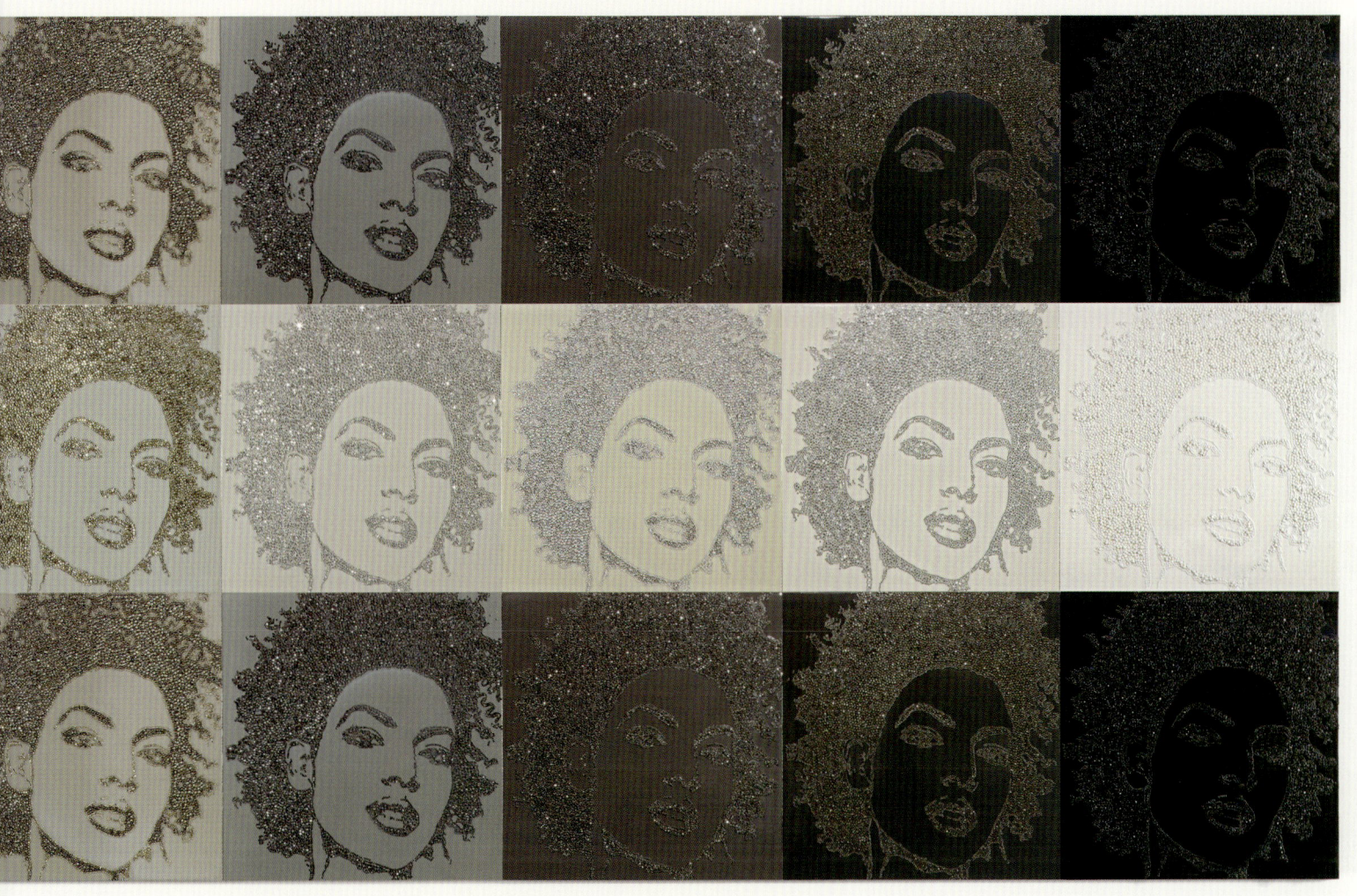
Mickalene Thomas, *Hair Portrait #20*, 2014, plastic rhinestones and acrylic on panel, 30 panels, 30 × 30 in. each, courtesy of the artist and Lehmann Maupin Gallery, New York and Hong Kong

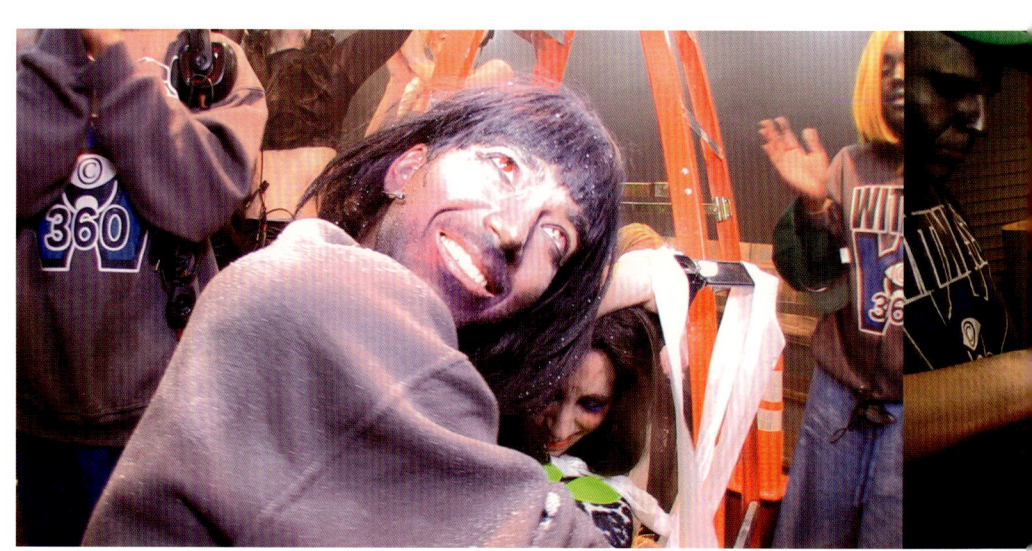

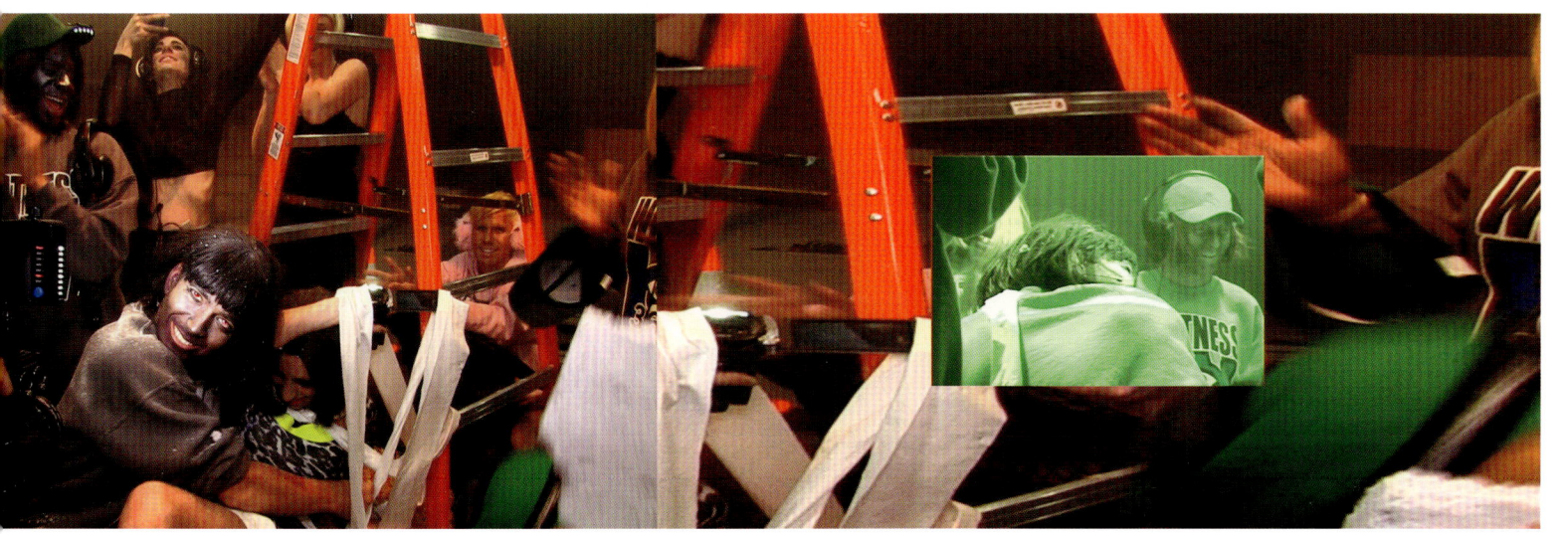

Ryan Trecartin, *Comma Boat* (still), 2013, three-channel HD video, 33:02 min., image courtesy of the artist, Regen Projects, Los Angeles, and Andrea Rosen Gallery, New York

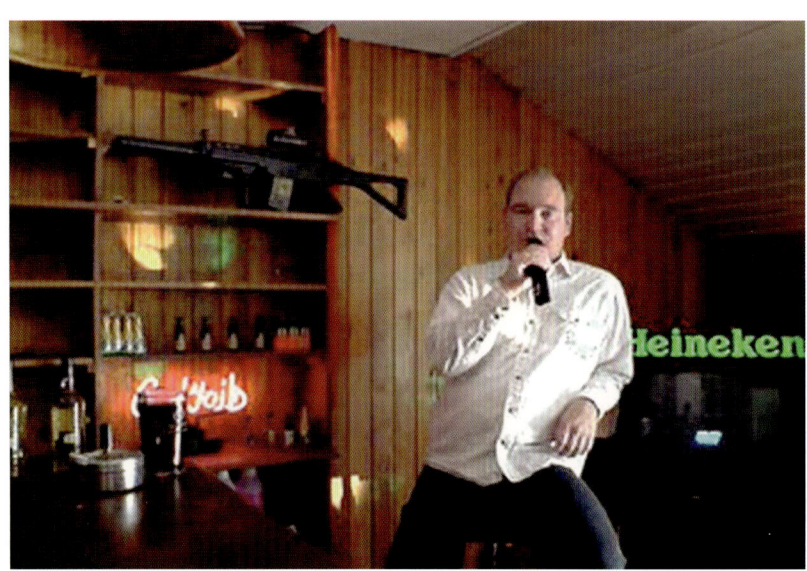

Amie Siegel, *My Way 2* (still), 2009, video, 12 min., courtesy of Simon Preston Gallery, New York

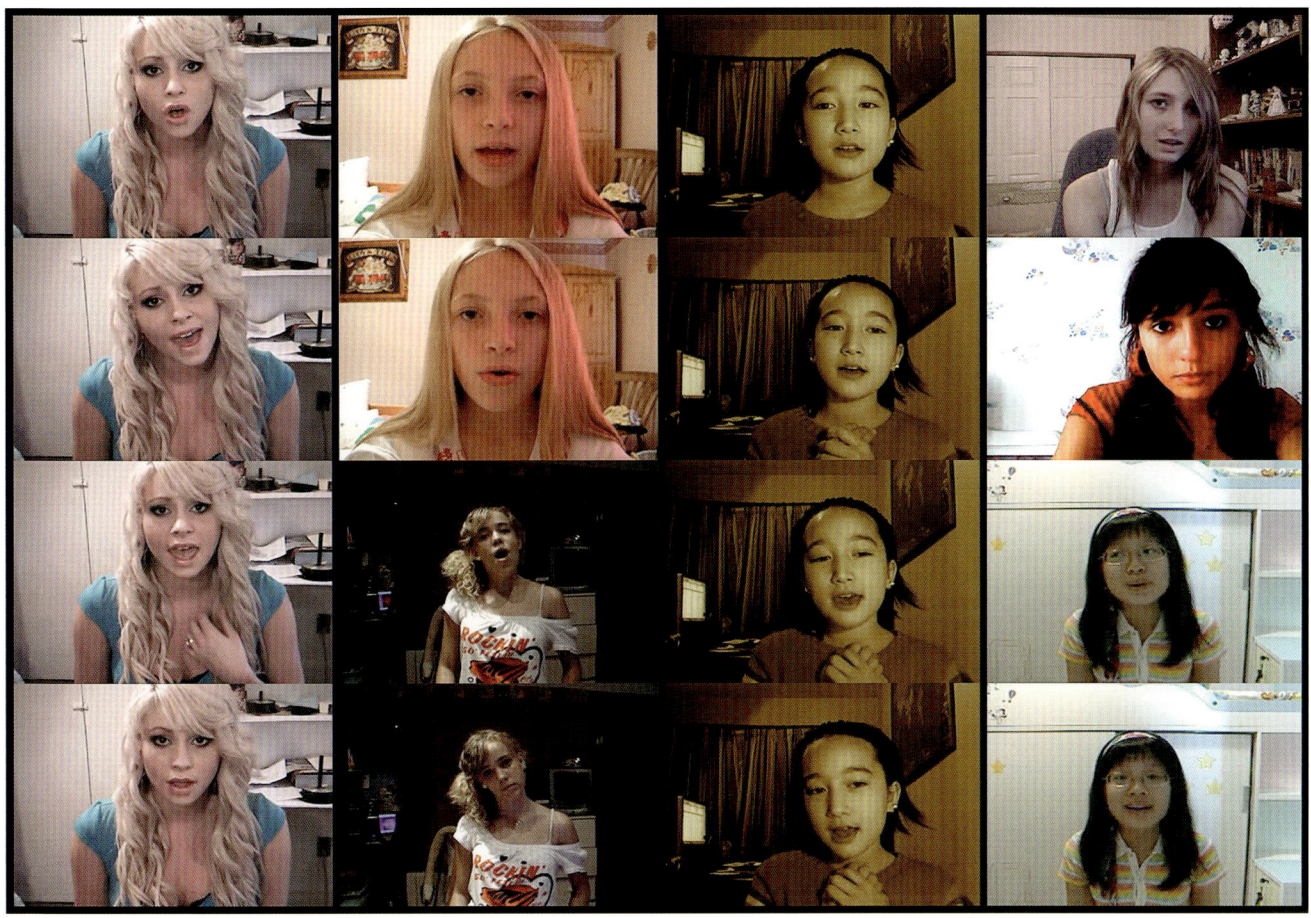

Amie Siegel, *My Way 1* (stills compilation), 2009, video, 9 min., courtesy of Simon Preston Gallery, New York

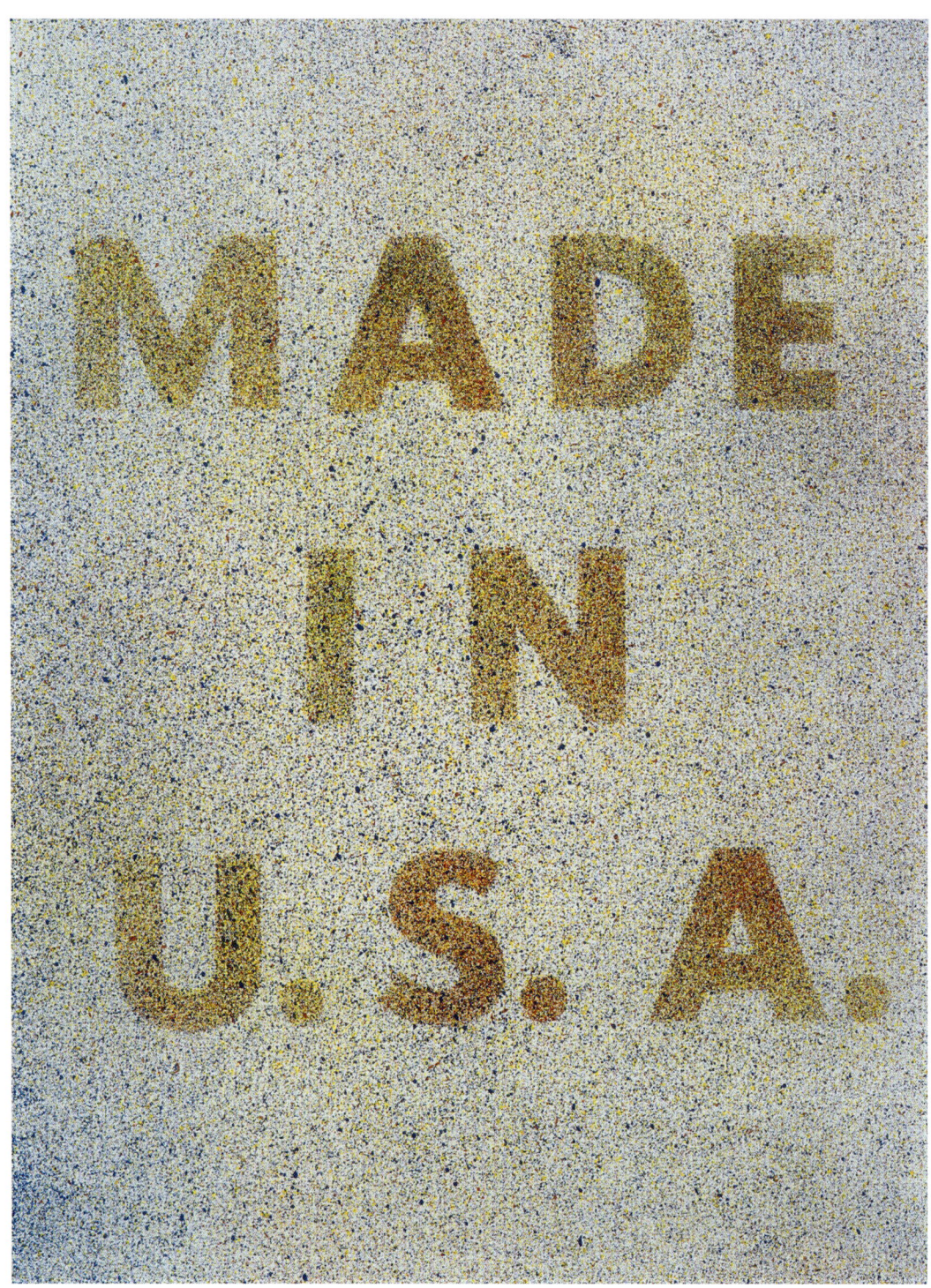

Ed Ruscha, *America Her Best Product*, 1974, lithograph, 31⅛ × 23½ in., Seattle Art Museum, Gift of the Lorillard Co. 75.73

Suggested Reading

1960s

Allan, Ken. "Ed Ruscha, Pop Art, and Spectatorship in 1960s Los Angeles." *The Art Bulletin*, vol. 92, no. 3 (2010): 231–249.

Allan, Ken, Lucy Bradnock, and Lisa Turvey. "For People Who Know the Difference: Defining the Pop Art Sixties." In *Pacific Standard Time: Los Angeles Art, 1945–1980*. Exh. cat. Los Angeles: Getty Research Institute and the J. Paul Getty Museum, 2011.

Bankowsky, Jack, Alison M. Gingeras, and Catherine Wood. *Pop Life: Art in a Material World*. London: Tate Publishing, 2009.

Evers, Elodie, Gregor Jansen, and Magdalena Holzhey. *Living with Pop*. Exh. cat. Cologne: Walther König, 2013.

Foster, Hal. *The First Pop Age: Painting and Subjectivity in the Art of Hamilton, Lichtenstein, Warhol, Richter, and Ruscha*. Princeton, NJ: Princeton University Press, 2012.

Francis, Mark, and Hal Foster. *Pop*. London: Phaidon, 2005.

Geldzahler, Henry, Hilton Kramer, Dore Ashton, Leo Steinberg, and Stanley Kunitz. "Pop Art Symposium at the Museum of Modern Art, December 13, 1962." *Arts Magazine* v. 37, no. 7 (April 1963): 36–45.

Geldzahler, Henry. *Pop Art 1955–70*. New York: The Museum of Modern Art International Council, 1985.

Harrison, Sylvia. *Pop Art and the Origins of Post-Modernism*. Cambridge: Cambridge University Press, 2001.

Lippard, Lucy. *Pop Art*. New York: Praeger, 1966.

Livingstone, Marco. *Pop Art: A Continuing History*. London: Thames & Hudson, 2000.

Lobel, Michael. *Image Duplicator: Roy Lichtenstein and the Emergence of Pop Art*. New Haven: Yale University Press, 2002.

Madoff, Steven Henry. *Pop Art: A Critical History*. Berkeley: University of California Press, 1997.

McCarthy, David. *Pop Art*. Cambridge & New York: Cambridge University Press, 2000.

Rosenblum, Robert. "Roy Lichtenstein and the Realist Revolt." *Metro* no. 8 (March 1963): 38–45.

Rosenthal, Mark. *Regarding Warhol: Sixty Artists, Fifty Years*. Exh. cat. New York: Metropolitan Museum of Art; New Haven: Yale University Press, 2012.

Whiting, Cécile. *A Taste for Pop: Pop Art, Gender, and Consumer Culture*. Cambridge: Cambridge University Press, 1997.

1980s

Bolton, Richard, ed. *The Contest of Meaning: Critical Histories in Photography*. Cambridge: MIT Press, 1989.

Butler, Cornelia H., and Lisa Gabrielle Mark. *WACK!: Art and the Feminist Revolution*. Exh. cat. Los Angeles: Museum of Contemporary Art; Cambridge: MIT Press, 2007.

Crimp, Douglas. *Pictures: An Exhibition of the Work of Troy Brauntuch, Jack Goldstein, Sherrie Levine, Robert Longo, Philip Smith*. Exh. cat. New York: Committee for the Visual Arts. 1977.

Eklund, Douglas. *The Pictures Generation, 1974–1984*. Exh. cat. New York: Metropolitan Museum of Art; New Haven: Yale University Press, 2009.

Ellegood, Anne. *Take It or Leave It: Institution, Image, Ideology*. Exh. cat. Los Angeles: Hammer Museum; New York: Delmonico Books/Prestel, 2014.

Evans, David. *Appropriation*. London: Whitechapel; Cambridge: MIT Press, 2009.

Goldstein, Ann, and Mary Jane Jacobs. *A Forest of Signs: Art in the Crisis of Representation*. Exh. cat. Los Angeles: The Museum of Contemporary Art; Cambridge: MIT Press, 1989.

Molesworth, Helen, Johanna Burton, and Claire Grace. *This Will Have Been: Art, Love, & Politics in the 1980s*. Exh. cat. Chicago: Museum of Contemporary Art Chicago; New Haven: Yale University Press, 2012.

Owens, Craig. *Beyond Recognition: Representation, Power and Culture*. Scott Bryson, et. al., ed. Berkeley: University of California Press, 1992.

Pearlman, Alison. *Unpackaging Art of the 1980s*. Chicago: University of Chicago Press, 2003.

Tromble, Meredith, and Lynn Hershman Leeson. *The Art and Films of Lynn Hershman Leeson: Secret Agents, Private I*. Exh. cat. Seattle: Henry Art Gallery, University of Washington; Berkeley: University of California Press, 2005.

2000s

Cabrera, Margarita, and Rita González. *Margarita Cabrera*. Exh. cat. New York: Sara Meltzer Gallery, 2008.

Diederichsen, Diedrich. *On (Surplus) Value in Art*. Rotterdam: Witte de With Publishers; Berlin: Sternberg Press, 2008.

Griffin, Tim, ed. "This Is Today: Pop After Pop." Special issue, *Artforum* 43, no. 2 (October 2004).

Harrison, Rachel, and Eric Banks. *Rachel Harrison: Museum With Walls*. Exh. cat. Frankfurt am Main: Portikus, 2010.

Lassry, Elad, et. al. *Elad Lassry*. Exh. cat. Zurich: JRP Ringier Kunstverlag, 2010.

Meckseper, Josephine. *Josephine Meckseper*. Exh. cat. New York: FLAG Art Foundation, 2011.

Meyer, Richard. *What Was Contemporary Art?* Cambridge: MIT Press, 2013.

Siegel, Amie, et. al. *Amie Siegel: Berlin-Remake*. Frankfurt am Main: Revolver, Archiv für Aktuelle Kunst, 2006.

Thomas, Mickalene, and Lisa Melandri. *Mickalene Thomas: Origin of the Universe*. Exh. cat. Santa Monica: Santa Monica Museum of Art, 2012.

Trecartin, Ryan, et. al. *Any Ever: Ryan Trecartin*. Exh. cat. New York: Skira Rizzoli Publications in association with Elizabeth Dee, 2011.

Voorhies, James. *On Symptoms of Cultural Industry*. North Adams, MA: Bureau for Open Culture, 2011.

Voorhies, James. *Seventh Dream of Teenage Heaven*. Columbus, OH: Bureau for Open Culture, 2011.

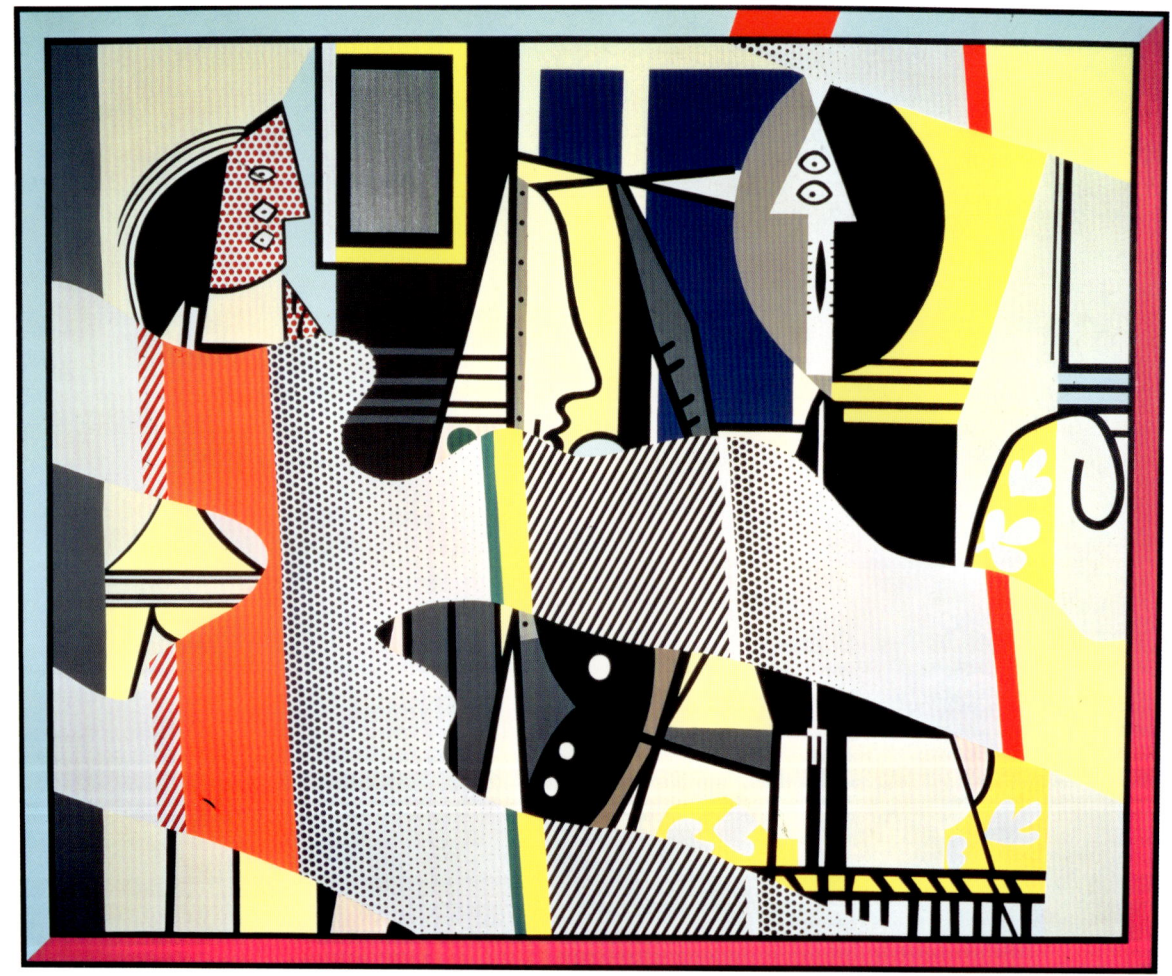

Roy Lichtenstein, *Reflections on Painter and Model*, 1990, oil and magna on canvas, 78 × 96 in., Collection of Richard and Elizabeth Hedreen

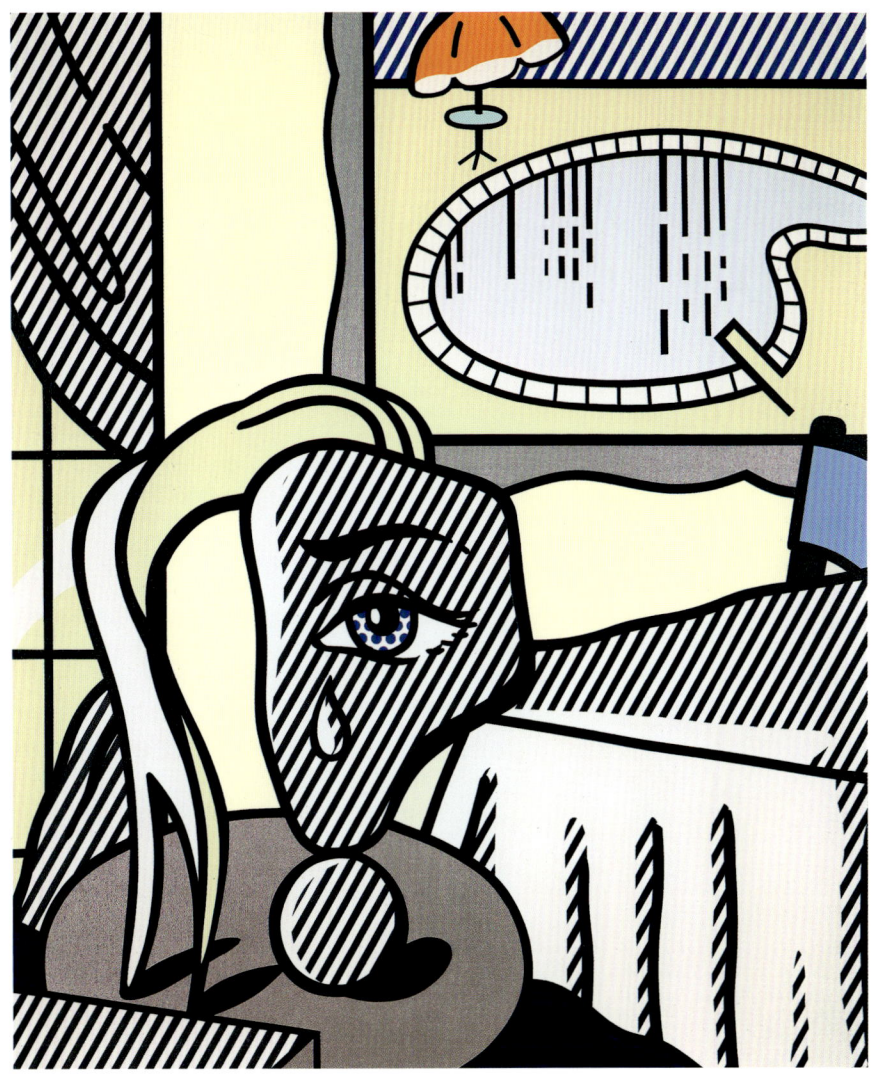

Roy Lichtenstein, *Interior with Swimming Pool*, 1992, oil and magna on canvas, 72 × 60 in., Janet Ketcham Collection

Guest Contributors

Ken Allan is Associate Professor of Art History in the Department of Fine Arts at Seattle University. His recent work on art in 1960s Los Angeles has been published in *The Art Bulletin*, *Art Journal*, the book *Pacific Standard Time: Los Angeles Art, 1945–1980* (Getty Publications), and the exhibition catalogue *The City Lost and Found: Capturing New York, Chicago and Los Angeles, 1960–1980* (The Art Institute of Chicago/Princeton University Art Museum).

Anne Ellegood has been the Senior Curator at the Hammer Museum in Los Angeles since 2009. Her recent projects include *Take It or Leave It: Institution, Image, Ideology* (coorganized with Johanna Burton), a group show that examined the overlapping strategies of appropriation and institutional critique in American art; an exhibition with Kelly Nipper; and Hammer Projects with Latifa Echakhch, Dara Friedman, and Sara VanDerBeek, among others. She is currently working on a solo exhibition with Laurie Anderson (2015) and the first retrospective of the work of Jimmie Durham in the United States (2017), as well as Hammer Projects with Francis Upritchard, Pedro Reyes, and Lily Van Der Stokker.

Elodie Evers studied cultural science and art history in Berlin and Montreal then completed the extra occupational course Cultures of the Curatorial at the Hochschule für Grafik und Buchkunst in Leipzig. She became Curator at the Kunsthalle Düsseldorf in 2009 and has organized exhibitions with Simon Evans, Matt Connors, Chris Martin, João Maria Gusmão & Pedro Paiva, and Hans-Peter Feldmann, among others, as well as the thematic group shows *Smart New World*, *Living with Pop: A Reproduction of Capitalist Realism*, and *A Void*.

Hal Foster is Townsend Martin Class of 1917 Professor of Art & Archaeology at Princeton University, where he also directs the Program in Media & Modernity. His many notable publications include *The Art-Architecture Complex* (Verso) and *The First Pop Age: Painting and Subjectivity in the Art of Hamilton, Lichtenstein, Warhol, Richter, and Ruscha* (Princeton University Press), as well as *Art since 1900* (Thames & Hudson), a coauthored textbook on twentieth-century art; *Prosthetic Gods* (October Books), which concerns the relation between modernism and psychoanalysis; and *Design and Crime* (Verso), a consideration of problems in contemporary art, architecture, and design.

Lynn Hershman Leeson, an acclaimed artist and filmmaker, has pioneered new technologies in her ongoing investigation of issues that are now recognized as key to the working of our society. She is a recipient of the 2014 Visionary Pioneers Award from Ars Electronica and the d.velop digital art Lifetime Achievement Award, as well as a Siggraph Lifetime Achievement Award, Eureka and Rainen Fellowships, a Prix Ars Electronica Grand Prize, and a John Simon Guggenheim Memorial Foundation Fellowship. Her artwork is featured in many celebrated private collections and such major public collections as the Museum of Modern Art in New York; Zentrum für Kunst und Medientechnologie in Karlsruhe, Germany; the Los Angeles County Museum of Art; Tate Modern in London; and the Hess Collection in Napa, California. A retrospective of her work, accompanied by a monograph, will take place at the ZKM Mediammuseum in December 2014.

Josephine Meckseper's noted works meld the aesthetic language of modernism with the formal language of commercial display. She received her MFA from the California Institute of the Arts. Her work has been shown in biennials and museum exhibitions worldwide and is in the permanent collections of numerous international museums, including the Museum of Modern Art, the Solomon R. Guggenheim Museum, and the Whitney Museum of American Art in New York; the Migros Museum in Zurich, Switzerland; and the Kunstmuseum in Stuttgart, Germany.

Richard Meyer is Robert and Ruth Halperin Professor in Art History at Stanford University. In 2013, he published *What Was Contemporary Art?* (MIT Press), a history of the idea of contemporary art in in early twentieth-century America, and *Art and Queer Culture* (Phaidon), a survey focusing on visual art and non-normative sexuality from the late nineteenth century to the present, coedited with Catherine Lord.

Mickalene Thomas is a distinguished multidisciplinary visual artist best known for combining art-historical, political, and pop-cultural references to create striking figurative and nonfigurative paintings. She received her MFA from Yale University, and holds a BFA from Pratt Institute. Thomas's work is collected by prominent museums and private collections nationally and internationally. She lives and works in Brooklyn, New York.

James Voorhies is a curator, art historian, and writer. He is the John R. and Barbara Robinson Family Director of the Carpenter Center for the Visual Arts at Harvard University. His writing has appeared in publications by *Texte zur Kunst*, *Frieze*, and Printed Matter, as well as numerous artist monographs and exhibition catalogues. He is the founder of Bureau for Open Culture, a nonprofit curatorial and publishing initiative that (from 2007 to 2014) collaborated with museums, universities, and foundations to make projects with contemporary artists and writers.

Exhibition Checklist

John Baldessari
American, born 1931

Kiss, Hair, Hands, 1986
Photogravure and aquatint on
BFK Rives paper
28¾ × 19¾ in. (73 × 50.2 cm)
Henry Art Gallery, University of
Washington, gift from the
Collection of Steven Johnson
and Walter Sudol, 97.316.4

Legs, Straw, Diver, 1986
Photogravure and aquatint on
BFK Rives paper
26⅛ × 19¾ in. (66.4 × 50.2 cm)
Henry Art Gallery, University of
Washington, gift from the
Collection of Steven Johnson
and Walter Sudol, 97.316.5

Margarita Cabrera
Mexican, born 1973

Battery Mixer, 2003
Vinyl, thread, metal, electric parts
10 × 7 × 10 in. (25.4 × 17.8 ×
25.4 cm)
Courtesy of the artist

Food Processor, 2003
Vinyl, thread, and appliance parts
14 × 10 × 8 in. (35.6 × 25.4 ×
20.3 cm)
Courtesy of the artist

Slow Cooker, 2003
Vinyl, thread, and appliance parts
13 × 8 × 10 in. (33 × 20.3 × 25.4 cm)
Courtesy of the artist

Vocho (Yellow), 2004
Vinyl, batting, thread, and car parts
60 × 72 × 156 in. (152.4 × 182.9 ×
396.2 cm)
Anne and William J. Hokin
Collection
Cover image, ill. pages 24–25

Cleaning Supplies, 2012
Vinyl and thread
14 × 10 × 14 in. (35.6 × 25.4 ×
35.6 cm)
Courtesy of the artist

John Chamberlain
American, 1927–2011

J.J.J.J., 1963
Mixed media
48 × 43 × 42 in. (121.9 × 109.2 ×
106.7 cm)
Private collection

Ultra Yahoo, 1967
Steel
54 × 59½ × 39 in. (137.2 × 151.1 ×
99.1 cm)
Private collection
Ill. page 42

High Tale, 1978
Painted and chromepainted steel
84½ × 25 × 32 in. (214.6 × 63.5 ×
81.3 cm)
Collection of Jeffrey and
Susan Brotman
Ill. page 43

Rachel Harrison
American, born 1966

Very Young Small, 2005
Handpainted cast resin with
acrylic and can of peas
16¾ × 16¼ × 9¼ in. (42.6 × 41.3 ×
23.5 cm)
Henry Art Gallery, University
of Washington, gift of David and
Tia Hoberman, 2008.225 AB
Ill. pages 28, 89

Robert Heinecken
American, 1931–2006

Waking Up In News America, 1986
Offset lithograph
26 × 38 in. (66 × 96.5 cm)
Seattle Art Museum, Gift of the
artist, 86.128

Recto/Verso, 1988
Series of 12 cibachrome
photograms
14 × 11 in. each (35.6 × 28 cm)
Seattle Art Museum, Richard E.
Lang Modern Acquisition Fund and
the Margaret E. Fuller Purchase
Fund, 90.31.1
Ill. page 80

Lynn Hershman Leeson
American, born 1941

Seduction, from *The Phantom
Limb* series, 1986
Gelatin silver photograph
20 × 24 in. (50.8 × 61 cm)
Seattle Art Museum, Gift of
Patterson Sims and Katy Homans,
95.78

TV Legs, from *The Phantom
Limb* series, 1987
Gelatin silver photograph
24 × 20 in. (61 × 50.8 cm)
Seattle Art Museum, Gift of
Rod Slemmons, 95.79
Ill. page 78

Robert Indiana
American, born 1928

The Electric EAT, 1964/2007
Polychrome aluminum, stainless
steel, and lightbulbs
78 × 78 × 7 in. (198.1 × 198.1 ×
17.8 cm)
Private collection
Ill. page 49

Martin Kippenberger
German, 1953–1997

*Nicht wegwerfen! (Kann man noch
für Nudelauflauf gebrauchen)*
(Don't Toss! [Can Still Be Used for
Noodle Casserole]), Berlin 1980
Offset
17 × 12 in. (43.2 × 30.5 cm)
Collection of Jeffrey and
Susan Brotman
Ill. page 88

9 Gründe, die Preise zu erhöhen
(9 Reasons to Raise Prices),
Cologne 1987
Silkscreen
32½ × 23 in. (82.6 × 58.4 cm)
Collection of Jeffrey and
Susan Brotman

Peter, Cologne 1987
Silkscreen
32½ × 23¾ in. (82.6 × 60.3 cm)
Collection of Jeffrey and
Susan Brotman

Untitled (Bucholz + Schipper),
Cologne 1990
Silkscreen
33 × 23⅜ in. (83.8 × 59.4 cm)
Collection of Jeffrey and
Susan Brotman

Jeff Koons
American, born 1955

Pink Panther, 1988
Porcelain on formica base
41 × 20½ × 19 in. (104.1 × 52.1 ×
48.3 cm)
Collection Museum of Contemporary Art Chicago, Gerald S. Elliott
Collection 1995.57
Ill. page 65

St. John the Baptist, 1988
Porcelain
56½ × 30 × 24½ in. (143.5 × 76.2 ×
62.2 cm)
Seattle Art Museum, Gift of the
Virginia and Bagley Wright Collection, in honor of the 75th Anniversary of the Seattle Art Museum,
2007.121
Ill. page 18

Barbara Kruger
American, born 1945

Untitled (Not cruel enough), 1997
Photographic silkscreen on vinyl
109 × 109 in. (276.9 × 276.9 cm)
The Museum of Contemporary Art,
Los Angeles, Gift of Vivian and
Hans Buehler
Ill. page 69

Elad Lassry
American, born 1977

Portrait, Purple, 2008
C-print, painted frame
10½ × 8½ × 1½ in. (26.7 × 21.6 ×
3.8 cm)
Collection of Kai Loebach
Ill. page 86 (top left)

Wolf (Blue), 2008
C-print, painted frame
11½ × 14½ × 1½ in. (29.2 × 36.8 ×
3.8 cm)
Courtesy of David Kordansky
and Mindy Shapiro, Los Angeles
Ill. page 86 (bottom right)

*Truffle Goat Cheese, Emmentaler,
Fork and Spoon*, 2010
C-print, painted frame
14 × 11½ × 1½ in. (35.6 × 29.2 ×
3.8 cm)
Courtesy of David Kordansky and
Mindy Shapiro, Los Angeles
Ill. pages 22, 87 (top left)

Woman (Painting), 2010
C-print, painted frame
14 × 11½ × 1½ in. (35.6 × 29.2 ×
3.8 cm)
Courtesy of David Kordansky and
Mindy Shapiro, Los Angeles
Ill. page 87 (bottom left)

Four Eggs, 2013
C-print, painted frame
14 × 11½ × 1½ in. (35.6 × 29.2 ×
3.8 cm)
Courtesy of David Kordansky and
Mindy Shapiro, Los Angeles
Ill. page 87 (right)

*Laminated Structure
(For Stage)*, 2013
Silver gelatin print on C-print,
painted frame
14 × 11½ × 1½ in. (35.6 × 29.2 ×
3.8 cm)
Courtesy of the artist and David
Kordansky Gallery, Los Angeles
Ill. page 86 (top right)

Wave 90046, 2013
Silver gelatin print, walnut frame
14 × 11½ × 1½ in. (35.6 × 29.2 ×
3.8 cm)
Courtesy of the artist and David
Kordansky Gallery, Los Angeles
Ill. page 86 (bottom left)

Roy Lichtenstein
American, 1923–1997

On, 1961
Oil on canvas
29 × 19 in. (73.7 × 48.3 cm)
Collection Simonyi
Endpaper image

Bratatat, 1962
Magna on canvas
46 × 34 in. (116.8 × 86.4 cm)
Collection Simonyi
Ill. page 2

Image Duplicator, 1963
Oil and magna on canvas
24 × 20 in. (61 × 50.8 cm)
Collection Simonyi
Endpaper image

Study for Vicki!, 1964
Oil and magna on paper
42 × 41½ in. (106.7 × 105.4 cm)
Seattle Art Museum, General Acquisition Fund, 75.102

Kiss V, 1964
Magna on canvas
36 × 36 in. (91.4 × 91.4 cm)
Collection Simonyi
Ill. page 40

Red Painting (Brush Stroke), 1965
Oil and magna on canvas
60 × 60 in. (152.4 × 152.4 cm)
Collection Simonyi
Ill. page 41

Varoom, 1965
Oil and magna on canvas
36 × 36 in. (91.4 × 91.4 cm)
Collection Simonyi
Ill. page 3

Reflections on Painter and Model, 1990
Oil and magna on canvas
78 × 96 in. (198.1 × 243.8 cm)
Collection of Richard and Elizabeth Hedreen
Ill. page 98

Interior with Swimming Pool, 1992
Oil and magna on canvas
72 × 60 in. (182.9 × 152.4 cm)
Janet Ketcham Collection
Ill. page 99

Josephine Meckseper
German, born 1964

American Mall, 2010
Mixed media
120 × 282 × 48 in. (304.8 × 716.3 × 121.9 cm)
Courtesy of Andrea Rosen Gallery, New York
Ill. pages 27, 56, 84–85

Claes Oldenburg
American (born Sweden), born 1929

Strong Arm, 1961
Plaster and enamel paint
43 × 42 in. (109.2 × 106.7 cm)
Collection of Barney A. Ebsworth
Ill. page 47

Giant Wedge of Pecan Pie, 1963
Muslin soaked in plaster over wire frame, wood, painted with enamel
15 × 21 × 50 in. (38.1 × 53.3 × 127 cm)
Seattle Art Museum, Promised gift of the Virginia and Bagley Wright Collection, in honor of the 75th Anniversary of the Seattle Art Museum
Ill. page 16

Baked Potato, 1966
Cast resin, painted with acrylic, Shenango China dish
4½ × 10½ × 7 in. (11.43 × 26.67 × 17.78 cm)
Seattle Art Museum, Gift of Sidney and Anne Gerber, 86.274.4
Ill. page 48

Drums–London (Soft Drum Set), 1966
Offset lithograph
24 × 35¼ in. (61 × 89.6 cm)
Seattle Art Museum, Gift of the Contemporary Art Council by exchange, 79.66

Model: Wingnut, Proposed Colossal Monument for Karlaplan, Stockholm, 1967
Wood relief with Liquitex paint
46⅜ × 48 × 12½ in. (31.8 × 117.8 × 121.9 cm)
Seattle Art Museum, Promised gift of the Virginia and Bagley Wright Collection, in honor of the 75th Anniversary of the Seattle Art Museum

Miniature Soft Drum Set, 1969
Canvas, stencil, spray painting
24¼ × 20 × 14 in. (61.6 × 50.8 × 35.6 cm)
Henry Art Gallery, University of Washington, Gift of Marc Selwyn, 2012.152 A–J

Geometric Mouse–Scale C, 1970–71
Aluminum and steel
24½ × 20 in. (62.2 × 50.8 cm)
Seattle Art Museum, Gift of the Robert B. and Honey Dootson Collection, 82.182

Ice Bag–Scale B, 1971
Programmed kinetic construction in aluminum, steel, nylon, fiberglass
40 × 48 × 48 in. (101.6 × 121.9 × 121.9 cm)
Seattle Art Museum, Gift of Mr. and Mrs. David E. Skinner, II, 84.224
Ill. page 17

Proposal for a Colossal Structure in the Form of a Sink Faucet— For Lake Union, Seattle, 1972
Offset color lithograph
27¾ × 21¾ in. (70.5 × 55.3 cm)
Seattle Art Museum, Gift of the Contemporary Art Council of the Seattle Art Museum, 72.79

Proposal for a Feasible Monument in the Form of Melting Butter, 1972
Watercolor and crayon on paper
14⅛ × 20 in. (35.9 × 50.8 cm)
Seattle Art Museum, Margaret E. Fuller Purchase Fund and Contemporary Art Council of the Seattle Art Museum, 75.34

M. Mouse (with) 1 Ear (equals) Tea Bag Blackboard Version (1965), 1973
Lithograph, screenprint, and hand dusting
9 × 12 in. (22.9 × 30.5 cm)
Seattle Art Museum, Gift of Robert Rauschenberg, 76.87.19

Nam June Paik
South Korean, 1932–2006

Attila the Hun, 1993
Mixed media
96½ × 39¾ × 80¾ in. (245.1 × 101 × 205.1 cm)
Collection of Jon Shirley
Ill. page 77

Raymond Pettibon
American, born 1957

No Title (Turning into a), 1980
Pen and ink on paper
17 × 20⅞ in. (43.2 × 53 cm)
Courtesy of the artist and Regen Projects, Los Angeles

No Title, 1981
Pen and ink on paper
15 × 11 in. (38.1 × 27.9 cm)
Courtesy of the artist and Regen Projects, Los Angeles

No Title (Vavoom in the), 1991
Ink on paper
17 × 20⅞ in. (43.2 × 53 cm)
Courtesy of the artist and Regen Projects, Los Angeles
Ill. page 6

No Title (They are hardly), 1997
Pen and ink on paper
11½ × 21½ in. (29.2 × 54.6 cm)
Courtesy of the artist and Regen Projects, Los Angeles

No Title (It could've been), 2003
Pen and ink on paper
19⅞ × 26⅛ in. (50.5 × 66.4 cm)
Courtesy of the artist and Regen Projects, Los Angeles

Richard Prince
American, born 1949

Untitled (Cowboys), 1980
Ektacolor print
27 × 40 in. (68.6 × 101.6 cm)
The Museum of Contemporary Art, Los Angeles, Purchased with funds provided by the National Endowment for the Arts, a Federal Agency, and Councilman Joel Wachs
Ill. pages 21, 67

Untitled (Girlfriend), 1993
Ektacolor print
64 × 44 in. (162.6 × 111.8 cm)
Private collection
Ill. page 66

Untitled (Girlfriend), 1993
Ektacolor print
64 × 44 in. (162.6 × 111.8 cm)
Private collection

Mel Ramos
American, born 1935

Devil Doll, 1963–64
Oil on canvas
50 × 44 in. (127 × 111.8 cm)
Louis K. Meisel Gallery
Ill. page 53

Moose, 1968
Oil on canvas
70¾ × 145 in. (179.7 × 368.3 cm)
Seattle Art Museum, Gift of Manuel Neri, 86.243

AC Annie, 1971
Offset lithograph
33¾ × 25⅛ in. (85.7 × 63.8 cm)
Los Angeles County Museum of Art, Gift of Michael Asher and Pamela Sue Allen, AC1997.200.9
Ill. page 62

Lola Cola, 1972
Offset lithograph
33¾ × 25⅛ in. (85.7 × 63.8 cm)
Los Angeles County Museum of Art, Gift of Michael Asher and Pamela Sue Allen, AC1997.200.8

David Robbins
American, born 1957

Talent, 1986–87
Photographs
18 photographs, 10 × 8 in. (25.4 × 20.32 cm) each
Seattle Art Museum, Purchased in honor of Peter Nesbett with a gift from Randi and Michael Hopkins, the Contemporary Arts Council, and the Modern Art Acquisition Fund, 98.31

James Rosenquist
American, born 1933

Dishes, 1964
Oil on canvas
50 × 60 in. (127 × 152.4 cm)
Seattle Art Museum, Promised gift of the Virginia and Bagley Wright Collection, in honor of the 75th Anniversary of the Seattle Art Museum
Ill. page 61

Edward Ruscha
American, born 1937

Damage, 1964
Oil on canvas
72 × 67 × 2 in. (182.9 × 170.2 × 5.1 cm)
Collection of Jeffrey and Susan Brotman
Ill. page 10

Vanishing Cream, 1973
Egg yolk on waterfall rayon
35⅞ × 40 in. (91.1 × 101.6 cm)
Seattle Art Museum, Promised gift of the Virginia and Bagley Wright Collection, in honor of the 75th Anniversary of the Seattle Art Museum
Ill. page 74

America Her Best Product, 1974
Lithograph
31⅜ × 23½ in. (79.7 × 59.7 cm)
Seattle Art Museum, Gift of the Lorillard Co., N.Y., 75.73
Ill. page 96

An Exhibition of Gasoline Powered Engines, 1993
Acrylic on linen
84 × 84 in. (213.4 × 213.4 cm)
Seattle Art Museum, Jeffrey and Susan Brotman, Mary Alice and Dick Cooley, Jane and David Davis, Robert Dootson, Lyn and Jerry Grinstein, Ann and John H. Hauberg, Mimi and Vinton Sommerville, Mary and Dean Thornton, Carol Wright, and the Margaret E. Fuller Purchase Fund, 98.52
Ill. page 75

Amie Siegel
American, born 1974

My Way 1, 2009
Video, color and sound
9 min.
Courtesy of the artist
Ill. page 95

My Way 2, 2009
Video, color and sound
12 min.
Courtesy of the artist
Ill. pages 31, 94

Rena Small
American, born 1954

Andy Warhol, from the *Artist's Hands* series, 1985
Silver gelatin print
9½ × 7½ in. (24.1 × 19 cm)
Seattle Art Museum

Wayne Thiebaud
American, born 1920

Bakery Counter, 1962
Oil on canvas
54⅞ × 71⅞ in. (139.4 × 182.6 cm)
Collection of Barney A. Ebsworth
Ill. page 51

Mickalene Thomas
American, born 1971

Hair Portrait #20, 2014
Plastic rhinestones and acrylic on panel
30 panels, 30 × 30 in. each (76.2 × 76.2 cm)
Courtesy of the artist and Lehmann Maupin Gallery, New York and Hong Kong
Ill. pages 38, 90–91

Ryan Trecartin
American, born 1981

Comma Boat, 2013
Three channel HD video, color and sound
33:02 min.
Courtesy of the artist and Regen Projects, Los Angeles
Ill. pages 92–93

Andy Warhol
American, 1928–1987

Double Elvis, 1963 / 1976
Silkscreen ink, synthetic polymer paint on canvas
Two panels, 82¼ × 59⅛ in. (208.9 × 150.2 cm) each
Seattle Art Museum, National Endowment for the Arts, PONCHO and the Seattle Art Museum Guild, 76.9
Ill. pages 14–15

Jackie, 1964
Synthetic polymer paint and silkscreen on canvas
20 × 16 in. (50.8 × 40.6 cm)
Jeffrey and Susan Brotman
Ill. page 44

Marilyn, 1967
Screenprint on paper
36 × 36 in. (91.4 × 91.4 cm)
Seattle Art Museum, Bequest of Kathryn L. Skinner, 2004.119
Ill. page 45

Flowers, 1970
Screenprint on paper
36 × 36 in. (91.4 × 91.4 cm)
Seattle Art Museum, Gift of Willard Wright, 91.42

Flowers, 1970
Screenprint on paper
36 × 36 in. (91.4 × 91.4 cm)
Seattle Art Museum, Bequest of Kathryn L. Skinner, 2004.120

Flowers, 1970
Screenprint on paper
36 × 36 in. (91.4 × 91.4 cm)
Seattle Art Museum, Bequest of Kathryn L. Skinner, 2004.121

Vote McGovern, 1972
Screenprint on Arches 88 paper
42 1/16 × 42 1/16 in. (106.8 × 106.8 cm)
Seattle Art Museum, Gift of the American Art Foundation, 79.87

Mao Tse Tung, 1972
Screenprint on Beckett High White paper
42 1/16 × 42 1/16 in. (106.8 × 106.8 cm)
Seattle Art Museum, Gift of the American Art Foundation, 79.91

Mick Jagger (#1), 1975
Screenprint on Arches Aquarelle paper
44 × 29¼ in. (111.7 × 74.3 cm)
Seattle Art Museum, Gift of the American Art Foundation, 79.88
Ill. page 36

Jane Lang Davis, 1976
Silkscreen ink, synthetic polymer paint on canvas
Two panels, 40 × 40 in. (101.6 × 101.6 cm) each
Seattle Art Museum, Gift of Mr. and Mrs. Richard E. Lang, 76.47 (left panel)
Collection of Jane Lang Davis (right panel)
Ill. page 71

Muhammed Ali, 1978
Screenprint on Strathmore Bristol paper
40 × 30 in. (101.6 × 76.2 cm)
Seattle Art Museum, Gift of the American Art Foundation, 79.90

Two White Mona Lisas, 1980
Silkscreen polymer on canvas
26½ × 40 in. (67.3 × 101.6 cm)
Collection of Ann P. Wyckoff
Ill. pages 72–73

Diamond Dust Shoes, 1980–81
Acrylic, silkscreen ink, and diamond dust on linen
49¾ × 42 in. (126.4 × 106.7 cm)
Janet Ketcham Collection
Ill. page 34

Tom Wesselmann
American, 1931–2004

Great American Nude No. 66, 1965
Oil and acrylic on canvas
73 × 73½ in. (185.4 × 186.7 cm)
Seattle Art Museum, Promised gift of the Virginia and Bagley Wright Collection, in honor of the 75th Anniversary of the Seattle Art Museum
Ill. page 63